FOREVER IS NOW

FOREVER IS NOW

By

WILDA LOWELL CONGER

AND

ELIZABETH CUSHMAN

THE CHRISTOPHER PUBLISHING HOUSE
BOSTON, U.S.A.

PRINTED IN THE UNITED STATES OF AMERICA

PROLOGUE

FROM DEATH TO LIFE
FROM FAILURE TO GLORY
FROM DARK SHADOWS TO SUNLIT PATHS
FROM PAIN TO JOY
WE HAVE WALKED WITH OUR MASTER ALL THE WAY
IN GRATITUDE TO HIM
AND WITH HOPE OTHERS SHALL FIND
COURAGE, FAITH, AND RELEASE THROUGH THESE TRUTHS
    OF SPIRIT
WE HUMBLY DEDICATE THIS BOOK

TABLE OF CONTENTS

FOREWORD

This is a heart-warming, soul-inspiring, beautifully written account of a mother's fellowship and communion with her departed son. This communion is not a mere remembrance, but a living relationship of the living with the living.

We must all die, and we do not know when we shall die. The inevitability of death and our uncertain hold on this life are the twin causes of a deep-seated anxiety concerning death.

Death makes a mockery of life in the long run. The prospect of death as a final end would destroy human values. The thought of death cannot ennoble this life unless, along with it, there is the thought of an imperishable life beyond death where personal values are preserved and enriched in accordance with God's purpose.

Wilda Conger has the gift of perceptive vision, and in the fifty-five messages from the spiritual world she is able to give to every bereaved soul the reassurance that what happens at death is that the eternal life enjoyed here and now by the Christian becomes a richer fellowship with Christ after death and that "neither death nor life—will be able to separate us from the love of God in Christ Jesus our Lord."

Lowell, her son, makes real the hope of the indescribable joy that is to come to all awakened souls when they pass over. "You must let them know," he says, "that earth is but a training school to improve latent faculties and to put into action soul-desires which are the motivating forces of existence."

The answer of Christianity to our hope concerning human destiny and our assurance concerning our beloved dead lies in the words of the Apostles' Creed; "I believe . . . in the communion of the Saints." The communications of Lowell to his mother are not carried out by one who is a medium, nor by one who has the ability to suspend her own self-consciousness and allow her departed son to speak or otherwise manifest his presence through her. There is no preoccupation with establishing communication with the departed, for communication is not the same thing as communion. Rather, we find to our comfort that we may have communion with the departed through a realization of their presence, but always in a way that acknowledges and does not try to circumvent the natural barrier that death sets up between the living and the dead.

New understanding and soul growth come to Wilda and Franklin as their son advances in the realm of spirit.

It is confidently expected that this growing awareness of the spiritual side of life will be communicated to the reader as he pursues this fascinating story.

Alfred W. Price

St. Stephens Church
Philadelphia

PREFACE

These pages contain the story of a mother and her son. I am the mother and the son is Lowell, who went on to the larger life at the age of fifteen. His passing came as a terrific shock to his father and me, for he was our greatest joy in life. Lowell's whole personality was one of whistling joy and radiant energy. A leader in youth activities, although not a brilliant student, he had a natural wisdom and a quickness of mind beyond his adolescent years. He was full of humor, and his mischievous nature often led him into trouble; he loved all people and every experience seemed an adventure to him. His irrepressible singing and laughter stand out vividly to those who knew him.

I should like to explain before progressing further that, for many years, I have had the gift of intuitive writing. I confess that in my younger days this ability to write messages "out of the air" was a source of embarrassment and even annoyance to me. In contrast to my youthful, pleasure-loving thoughts, I was astounded by my compulsion to write such phrases as "There is no death" and "All life is one." Furthermore, a frightening awareness often came to me that my duty would be to voice the truth of the continuity of life to my world. Absorbed in worldly interests and dreams, I tried for years to ignore these inner urgings and their responsibility which my best self uncomfortably recognized. However, in more recent years and since I have learned to dedicate my life as well as my writings to God and His purposes, much comfort and inspiration have come to me through messages from the higher planes.

11

A few weeks after Lowell's death, messages from an unknown spirit began to be given to me as a solace and a guide in my grief. Following this time of preparation came the beautiful experience of hearing directly from my son, and for twenty-five years now I have many times and in many places scribbled on paper words and sentences from Lowell. They usually begin with an insistent pulsing in my mind of "Mom, Mom, Mom," and when I start writing, the words seem to pour out to me very rapidly, much more rapidly than one normally writes. In fact, the messages appear to be dictated to my inner mind at a very fast pace, and certainly through no conscious thought of my own.

Lowell's writings always seemed to me merely of personal interest and help, and, for some reason, I seldom reread many of them. Even though my worldly self at times questioned their authenticity, still, I carefully kept most of them over the years. They have been tucked away in notebooks, boxes, and drawers until recently when I gathered them all together. On putting them in chronological order and reading them that way for the first time, I discovered that they contain not only an amazing continuity but also a dramatic story. One reads therein of the growth of the soul of a young boy into a soul of spiritual maturity and Christlike beauty.

From the facts we have given her, Elizabeth Cushman has written the connective and autobiographical material. This part is in regular type in contrast to the messages which appear in italics. A few names in this book are marked with asterisks. These are false names used to disguise identity where possible embarrassment might be caused. All other names are true to life. My husband's memory for dates and details has been essential. In addition, his judgment and patience have been invaluable in editorial and advisory capacities.

As to the messages themselves, their choice of words and even the subject matter definitely are not mine. I used to think they were given to me to help ease a mother's loneliness and as a personal guide in the spiritual life. However, after serious thought and prayer, I came to the conclusion that they are meant for a wider purpose than I had formerly realized. Since, in the above sense, the messages are not mine, surely they are not mine to hoard. Their truths are universal; therefore, I offer Lowell's words to all who are searching for truth and light, especially to those bewildered souls who are dreading or rebelling against separation from loved ones.

Forever Is Now

1

LOWELL IS NOT LOST

In 1936, while we were vacationing in Maine, our only
child, Lowell, was called into the next world.

We know now that God heard our stricken cry. He answered, upheld us, and breathed His peace into our hearts.
Several weeks after the Boy Scout funeral at Arlington
Cemetery, an emotional reaction occurred. In complete despair from grief and too much pondering, I took the car
and broke away to be alone in my fight to understand. As
I drove faster and faster, I cried out;

"Lowell, I am coming to you."

Feeling a compulsion to drive over a cliff at the side of
the road, with increasing speed, I headed toward it. Suddenly, words of authority ringing in my consciousness commanded;

"Stop this car, you will never find your boy this way.
Go home, this is selfishness."

The car skidded as I turned away from the cliff and
miraculously came to a stop. As if led by an invisible power,
I drove home sobbing in hysteria. When Franklin, my husband, came running out to meet me, I cried out;

"Give me a pencil quickly!"

Puzzled by my request, he nevertheless brought me a
pencil and paper and, still hysterical, I threw myself on the

grass to write the following message, which contained the first words about my son to come through from the next world:

Washington, D. C.
October 17, 1936

"Earth life cannot be as one desires, but is law fulfilling itself. Trials and suffering need not be darkness but can be pathways leading into a new consciousness.

"Do not grieve for Lowell. Look back on happy memories. Know that these shall all be relived, more intensified, more vitally real, more spiritually perfect. You cannot understand now. Do not think so hard, for it tears you apart and makes you unfit to hear the still, small voice which comes when you are peaceful and quietly receptive. This voice is the beginning of a greater realization which will come to you both in time. Blind trust, love and serene faith in all that is good will sustain you during this abrupt separation.

"Lowell is not lost to you nor to humanity. He is not dead nor waveringly searching for earth-bound connections. He is securely, serenely ensconced in everlasting love. He is not bewildered. He still loves you and wants to reach out a hand when your grief overcomes you, but it is not the time for his reaching across. He must first become reconciled to Supreme Ideals. He must study the precepts of spiritual awakening. His keen mind has a long way to go before he can reach over and answer your questions. Your grief merely bewilders him, your faith and trust give him poise and radiant happiness. His work will be far bigger and more vital than any can be on earth. Do not retard its beginning and increasing usefulness by injecting personal

grief or bewilderment into it. Seek to live at the highest
level you know in your present state.

"Do not wait for time to heal. Your own service, day by
day, just as you are now trying to give it, will heal your
tears. I will help you. I will care for Lowell's spirit until
he unfolds his own wings of truth and rises to his true place
in the universe."

This first message which came to me in my extremity
not only helped to heal my shattered emotional state but
restored me to a more natural calmness of heart and mind.
In the early weeks after Lowell's passing and before I had
reached the breaking point, I had been held in an almost
abnormal state of suspension. We all know that this is a
fairly common human experience after a great shock or
loss. Our loving Father dulls our sense of reality at such
times, in addition to giving us a strength beyond our usual
capacity. "The Lord is nigh unto them who call upon
Him."

I would stress, however, that at this time our lives were
not fully committed to God. Neither Franklin nor I were
experienced in prayer or in the joy and strength of the inner
life. We called ourselves Christians but certainly had never
put real thought or emphasis on the spiritual side of life.
Lowell's spirit now began to lead us toward clearer understanding.

Following the inspiration and beneficial effects of this
message, we began to feel a new sense of direction in our
lives. No longer did we question Lowell's leaving us. In
fact, we understood that he had not left us and that he
would be with us forever.

Now we could make plans for the future. We three had
always loved California, so Franklin and I decided to make

our home there. Having rented our Washington house, we drove across the country, arriving in Coronado in early December. Throughout the long trip we seemed to feel the joy of Lowell's boyish spirit. Because of this we were happy and could rejoice, for we sensed that we had made the right decision and that we were pleasing him.

2

THE VEIL IS THIN

The second message, which follows, came to me before we left Washington. As it is read, perhaps my satisfaction that our son was happy and serving God may be appreciated.

Washington, D. C.
October 30, 1936

"Your child is making more than satisfactory adjustment to his new phase of life. He readily grasped the ideas necessary to arise from his state of emotional lassitude. He has rested; because you on earth did not unduly retard him by too much grief and rebellion to the immutable laws of succession, he has done better than the average spirit.

"He had no idea where he was when he awoke. All his pain, his ear trouble, and his operations seemed like a dream to him. His awakening was so natural that he experienced little bewilderment. His spiritual keenness has already attracted a circle of kindred spirits. He is with a group of workers searching for children who are maladjusted to life's problems. They seek, through sense vibration, children whose lives have been influenced by people not understanding truth and harmony. Older spirits will teach Lowell how to send suggestions and impulses into these children, that their minds may be awakened to right thinking. He is especially fitted to roam back to earth. His gay, winning spirit makes him accessible to right contacts.

On these earth wanderings, it will be easy for you to feel his spirit and to be in close touch with his work. You can help him. He will lead children to you, and your own light will attract them. Therefore, you will not need children of your own, because the mother-instinct will become universalized in your love for children who will be influenced by Lowell.

"*The veil is thin. The way is simple. The air is charged with mental vibrations. You could not fail to catch some of these, for you are closely attuned to many minds on this side. When you are ready, I will tell you more.*

"*Fear not loneliness. It is the quiet which precedes a more intense understanding and personal contact. Loneliness is the gateway to the indrawing of truth which will help your understanding.*"

Having been told this October day that we would have many children and young people in our life, I mention my nephew, Junie, as one example. He was born two years after Lowell, and the two boys were close companions. Junie spent several summers in Maine with us, and we have always been linked by a strong bond of love. After Lowell's passing, Junie came to us and unforgettably said:

"I'd like to try to take Lowell's place and to be as much of a son to you as I can."

This he has done in heart-warming fashion, and ours is one of life's richest relationships. Furthermore, we have often been aware of Lowell's influence working in and through Junie.

3

TIME OF DISCOURAGEMENT

At the period of the next two writings I was discouraged, full of conflict and troubled for many reasons. We were trying to adjust to an entirely new way of life, not only to life without Lowell but to life with Franklin in retirement, for in July he had been placed on inactive duty by the Navy. With our greatly reduced income, we were still heavily burdened by doctors' bills and other expenses from Lowell's illness and death. Thus, financial and practical problems seemed to be engulfing us. As I look back, I can see that I was desperately in need of spiritual help and that my son was trying to lift me to a higher and more serene level.

Lowell's joy was telling me not to be so serious. His peaceful adjustment was showing me that my growth, too, must be natural and unforced. He was trying to lift me and sometimes, amidst discord and confusion, I felt myself being pulled in a way beyond human understanding.

Coronado, California
January 10, 1937

"Lowell finds it difficult to express himself, but he is rapidly learning. He is such an excellent channel that he will gradually become an interpreter for many souls. He is receptive, versatile, and idealistic. His fun and irresistible gaiety are easily controlled and directed. He is building memories into materialization of spiritual expression. He takes a memory from earth experience and turns it into a

symbol, and then it becomes a permanent part of his aura. His childhood was happy and his symbols are bright with color and light. When he has worked them out, they will become a part of him in such a flexible form that he can inject them into your physical world. In other words, from their spiritual form they will again become physical or material.

"Every good thought you think is a spiritual bond with your child's new set of symbols. How better can I express it? You two are working in cooperation, he from the spiritual through to the material, you, from the material through to the psychic and spiritual. You help each other. He needs you and you need him. You are becoming, and will increasingly become, closer than you ever would have been had he remained on earth.

"He is a connecting link to a higher life which will enable you to help others. When you become discouraged, embittered or too absorbed in material sensation, you lose this finer contact. You cannot always stay on the same high spiritual level; sometimes you slip back. That is natural and to be expected. You are of the world and you must enjoy the things of the world, but you cannot find happiness without the high guiding star of your guardian angel. You have such a spirit who responds when you need him. Therefore, call and say:

" 'Oh! spirit, who is meant to guide my destiny, speak from your sphere to comfort, bless and direct me this day.' "

Coronado, California
February 5, 1937

"I am ready to relay words of encouragement from your spirit-child who stands close beside you now radiating warmth and love to you and Franklin.

"Lowell is radiantly happy. His spiritual progress has been excellent. He is the same carefree boy who needs to be disciplined occasionally here as he did in your life, but he has learned much! His kindness to less developed and less sensitive fellow-spirits has been exceptional.

"He misses you and earth connections at times. When he feels the urge, he can come close to you, and, as you feel his influence, he is happier. He believes you often realize he wants to tell you things. When you are unhappy or when inharmony exists, he knows you are disturbed. He can tell by color and vibration when you are happy, in spiritual harmony and developing along the right lines. When there is discord, cloudiness appears to dull the colors of your aura.

"Try to think of Lowell as a sweet chord of music which soothes and comforts you when life's discords become too wearing. He senses, rather than sees, your human needs. He wants to help, but has not as yet been trained to make direct communication with you.

"You must learn to relax. Not until you have learned physical, mental and spiritual relaxation can you begin to develop your creative gifts. There is tension and unsettled thought all around you. Ask God to direct a strong current of Love, Patience and Faith into your being. His smile is ever on those who turn to Him and ask. He never fails.

"Affirm: 'God alone can supply that which we lack to live our lives in complete understanding and harmony. We ask and believe that God will supply enough of courage, love and faith to enable us to live our lives to their fullest spiritual significance. This we ask, in His name, each night and as each new day dawns.'"

4

YELLOW JONQUILS

The day before Lowell's sixteenth birthday was a momentous day in my life. In the midst of writing helpful words from my spirit-friend, Lowell himself interrupted to give me his first words from the other side. To have this message from my son, to recognize his boyish style of expression, to sense his exuberance, his gaiety and his excitement was thrilling beyond description. As so often happens in life, this wonderful experience came at a time of anguish and distress. Despite all assurances, the sharp pain of human longing swept over me as Lowell's birthday approached. Furthermore, my husband who had long struggled against alcoholism was now reaching a nightmarish climax of this disease.

For about five months after Lowell's death, Franklin continued a period of non-drinking which had begun a few months earlier. Grief-stricken, also extremely nervous because of his long-standing desire for alcohol, he nevertheless refused to drink during those first months without Lowell. Anyone who has had any experience with the power of alcohol will appreciate the difficulty of my husband's struggle to stand by me at our time of heartbreak, for, if ever one addicted to alcohol feels the need of drink, it is at such a time.

Through very unfortunate circumstances Franklin allowed himself to accept a glass of wine one night in mid-February. That one little drink set aside all good intentions and began, for the first time, months of really intensive drinking. Grief over losing his only child now accentuated itself and he appeared to have lost all incentive to control the drinking which offered release from his anguished emotions.

When Lowell's words came to me during my writing the day before his birthday, great changes were being initiated in our lives. A few weeks later I came in contact with a dedicated group of Christians, a thrilling prayer fellowship. We also met Mary and Bob Harris, who were to become vital influences in our lives.

Acutely worried about Franklin and about our finances, which were in a deplorable state, I was at a very low ebb. Finally an ad in the newspaper produced a faint hope. "Put alcaban in his coffee," I read; whereupon, I immediately went out to find a drugstore. Timidly I asked the handsome, smiling clerk:

"Do you have alcaban?"

In a straightforward and oddly compelling manner the clerk answered my question with another:

"Is your husband an alcoholic?"

Embarrassed to admit such a fact to a stranger, I mumbled:

"Well, he drinks sometimes."

Now my original query was answered.

"No, I do not have alcaban, but I have something better. Have you ever tried the love of God?"

Astonished by this turn in the conversation, I began to think that the young man with the vitally alive eyes must be a bit queer. I point out that in 1937 little general information or constructive help was available for alcoholism; neither was it fashionable nor customary to refer casually to one's spiritual life. "Alcoholics Anonymous" was just being established, and the impact of referring to the love of God as a therapeutic measure was more startling than it would be today.

Regardless of my misgivings, I stayed to hear more. Calmly and with little show of emotion, my new friend told me his own story of bitter defeat and then true victory over alcohol through fellowship in prayer. His life had appeared to be in ruins. Having wrecked his car and lost his job through drinking, knowing his wife's decision to leave him, yet he had been able to "come to himself" like the prodigal son. Through honest surrender to God and prayer, he was restored to his rightful place of sonship and was rewarded with the abundance of his father's love. This love he was now expressing in concrete form as he sought to bring others to his Source of help. Incidentally, his is a genuine success story in material as well as spiritual realms. At the time of this writing, he is the mayor of a large western city and ranked as one of the outstanding mayors in the country, but his greatest success lies in his continuing influence in quietly bringing men to God.

After telling me of his experiences, he invited me to come to his home; in fact, he said, that evening a group meeting was being held there. In my excitement I forgot all about alcaban and rushed home to report my adventure to my sister, May, who was visiting us. Her enthusiasm encouraged me and strengthened my own belief which had unconsciously absorbed some of the contagious faith of the drugstore clerk.

May and I decided to go to the meeting that same night, and we surprised ourselves by talking freely of our problems. Never had I felt such love as I sensed there in that room. Another couple with more experience was reached by telephone and we were impressed that they both got dressed and came right over regardless of the fact that they had been tired and gone to bed early. The group had only one desire, to help us or anyone else in need who came to it as a channel for God's love. Being inexperienced in true dedication, I was amazed that nothing was expected in return. These people longed to do everything possible for us out of love and gratitude to God for what He had done for them. This was my first introduction to teamwork, to group prayer and to the power of relinquishment.

We all prayed together and gave the problem to God. Suddenly I felt miraculously free from worry. I am sure that I also assimilated some of the confidence and faith evinced in that little group. I went home to sleep soundly for the first time in weeks, feeling sure that we would be helped.

I was forewarned not to have a set pattern in my mind as to how God would answer. I was to believe only one fact, that He would surely answer. Keeping in contact with this group, I learned more about prayer and surrender, more about faith. I exulted, for Franklin seemed better for a while. Then came days of real testing when his condition worsened perceptibly. Stubbornly I clung to my new-found friends and my new-born faith.

One afternoon a lovely, dedicated, young woman from the group came to see us. Although she was full of Christ's love and had much more spiritual experience than I, she was a little frightened and nervous because drinking was entirely outside her knowledge. However, in spite of his seeming inability to comprehend, she talked to Franklin of God's love and power; later, she suggested he kneel to pray with her. To my surprise, he knelt beside her as she prayed, and I am convinced that through her prayer Franklin's spirit was reached. I can add that something also happened in those moments which gave me strength and courage to believe more fully.

I have written of these early days of spiritual experience in detail because I think it important to stress the value of prayer fellowship, of sharing problems and of surrendering everything to God. I have given a concrete example of the above in my own life, and I can testify to the sense of relief and to the definite help which followed.

The many prayers for us were indeed heard. In spite of outward appearances, God's power was already leading us to His answer for us. The following message asks me to read in the Scriptures, "Now is the accepted time; now is the day of salvation." Obviously, "now" refers to the beginning of my husband's healing and the verse was intended, as it did in great measure, to strengthen my own faith in this period when no improvement was yet visible. A revealing fact is that at this juncture, shortly before making the spiritual contacts mentioned, I even had difficulty in finding among our possessions a Bible in which to read the suggested Second Corinthians 6:2. However, find one I finally did, and that verse with its meaning in our lives will never be forgotten.

Coronado, California
May 14, 1937

"Memory is coming through—have patience—it will gain momentum with practice. Yes, Lowell realizes earth connections as you often comprehend a dream, yet they cannot seem important to him because he is in reality now. Dreams are wonderful to remember, especially happy ones, but they do not deviate our actions from channels where intelligent reality is needed.

"Your boy is a fine example of retrospective, unconscious

happiness. He has carried his gay, loving, sparkling ego and personal magnetism into this world, just as he carried it daily in your life. You couldn't wish him back, not if you saw him and understood. Your peaceful adjustment has come only because your real self senses this. You know in your heart that God's laws, God's purposes and God's ways of fulfilling great principles are always just and good, even though earthly or unheeding eyes do not see. It is not wise for you to draw your boy back too often or else you will retard his development. Your own development is keeping step with his, even though you cannot realize it. The spiritual tie between you is cosmic and irrevocably sealed through eternity from one life to another. It is going to change form many times, but it is always love—love burned and cleansed by self-sacrifice, infinite Love.

"Be part of eternal reconciliation, bend and sway with grace as the birch tree bends with the wind. Follow the tides of life as the path follows the wind sweeping and whisking across a wheat field. Lean toward the light, for from it comes life and vigor. From darkness comes soothing rest and a fresh vitality to meet the new dawn. Darkness is sometimes a preparation for the glory to follow. Pride may rebel, but pride does not change the tempest or the fury, it only wrecks its sore heart upon the rocks.

"Give, give, give all you have to life. Glorify it, capture its heights of ecstasy, its shadows of poignancy and its hillside slopes which can roll one into flat, hard valleys or lift one up to behold rare vistas. Your greatest life work is yet to come. Believe in yourself and in nature's intuitive warnings and urgings.

"No doctor, no nurse, no medicine will cure Franklin. His mind must be freed from self-condemnation. Yes, go away and leave him to work out his own problems. Relax, *rejoice. You cannot keep your own from you any more than you can keep your own with you. Read Second Corinthians 6:2. It will comfort you. 'For he saith, I have heard thee in a time accepted, and in the day of salvation have I succoured thee. Behold, now is the accepted time, now is the day of salvation.' "*

INTERRUPTION

"Mom, Mom, Mom, I am calling you, can you hear me? I know you so well. I remember it all. It was like a dream, but I am here. I am well now and happy, and so glad to talk to you. Don't miss me on my birthday, for I am going to be with you all day, so near that I can feel your breath. You will have a surprise. You will be as happy as I am. You wait and see. No, this is not your imagination, this is me, really! I am so excited. Oh mother, I love you and Daddy. Don't worry about Daddy."

Lowell's sixteenth birthday proved to be as happy as he had promised. It also contained the delightful surprise which he said would be forthcoming. To explain the surprise, I must first tell a little anecdote about Lowell. Similar tales are available from the youth of all scheming, mischievous boys. The report card exhibiting low marks is a familiar part of the plot. Lowell and I both loved yellow jonquils, and one spring day he had approached me holding a bunch behind his back and saying with his quick little smile:

"Mom, I thought these looked like you."

My pleased surprise over this lovely gift of flowers turned, of course, slightly rueful after the second gift, the report card, was tendered. However, this made a good, if typical, story of adolescence, and we all enjoyed it.

Lowell was now in the next world, but he was able to present me with yellow jonquils once again on his sixteenth birthday. That was my surprise, and it happened in the following manner. His cousin, Jackie, a week younger, came to see me and most unexpectedly brought me a bunch of Lowell's favorite flowers. Jackie's mother was as amazed as I by this marked departure from the usual teen-age routine. One might say "mere imagination" or "mere coincidence" or think me too credulous. Nevertheless, I know with an inner knowing beyond proof that an impulse from Lowell led Jackie to bring me yellow jonquils that day. This in no way detracts from Jackie's kindness and love. To the contrary, our world would be a much happier one if only more of us were sensitive enough and wise enough to follow the loving impulses which come to us. I should add that, to this day whenever I see yellow jonquils a feeling of great joy enfolds me.

5

TRANSFORMING LOVE

The spring and summer months were for me a time of change and growth. They were weeks of fluctuations in faith, but also of serious thought and earnest practice of prayer. Obviously we were going through a gradual process of preparation for healing and for future service.

Before writing the message which follows, I had been out on the golf course trying rather unsuccessfully to play that tantalizing game. With a happy thrill of recognition, I suddenly realized that Lowell was right there with me. Unlike his mother, he had a good deal of ability in the game and had often played with his father in the old days. On this lovely July day, I could almost hear him say in his laughing, teasing way, "Relax, Mom, swing and relax." To my amazement, I was immediately able to follow his good advice and to play a much better game than usual the rest of the day.

Coronado, California
July 2, 1937

"Yes, Mom, I was with you on the golf course today. You miss me too much and get too discouraged. Everything will be all right, you will have me always. Just the thoughts between us are powerful.

"I am learning about vibration, color and harmony. You are clear to me, clearer than anything else on earth. When I feel you wavering, I come. Don't worry about Pop so

much. He knows I can help him, but we want him to help
himself. He must understand that there are forces behind
him which will turn his way when he asks and believes
more fully.

"We here are learning gradually. Soon we can experiment more with human forces, but we are learning now
about material forces which come into being from the
spiritual. It is hard to explain what I mean, but your
thoughts make material manifestations. Your grief is like a
fog which shuts out many things between us. Try to be
happy. Go and buy some new hats, Mom, play golf, have
fun. You wonder about me so much that I am going to tell
you a secret. I am going to have a big surprise for you.
You and Dad will scarcely believe I did it. This place is
much better than even the Maine woods, or Alice Deal
School, or any place. I am building something—I am spirit-
ualizing your homecoming, but it will take years to perfect
it.

"I didn't mind changing into my new self, although I
was surprised. You were very good to me there, and when
I want to feel your presence now I merely have to think
to be with you. Our minds are our bodies. There is no
distance, we are everywhere. Please be happy, and Daddy
too. He needs to try to let me enter into his aura, he shuts
me out sometimes. He is afraid when I try to talk to his
mind, but he feels me near. I want to show him a bright
light to follow so that he will come out of the darkness
which surrounds him. Can't he feel brightness burning
sometimes, telling him what to do? He wants to stop earthly
mistakes, but he doesn't know how to start. He is lost. You
help him, Mom, and soon you will be glad about everything. I love you, Mom. I love you even more than when

I was on earth. I love the whole world, everything is so beautiful."

Lowell's reference here to his father's problem makes this seem an appropriate place for Franklin to tell, in his own way, the story of his struggle against alcoholism.

"My increasing addiction to alcohol and my consequent desperate condition have already been mentioned, but the extent of my degradation has not been sufficiently touched upon to give a true picture of my predicament. After many years of intermittent drinking, I had suddenly reached a point of no longer caring, a point of no control. Actually, during those last months, I drank to such excess that I was under the influence of liquor a large part of each day. My drunken condition necessitated that, night after night, I be under the care of a male nurse. My ensuing remorse and self-loathing were such agony that my self-respect and desire to live were being relentlessly destroyed. Having succumbed to my ruthless enemy, I was now in his power and thus incapable of helping myself. Always before I had been able to regulate my drinking and could stop whenever I wanted, but now that was all changed. Alcohol was an abomination to me, yet I had become its slave. The escape from reality which it provided was now a necessity. I was indeed lost.

"In August of 1937 I finally consented to go to a sanitarium for treatment. All credit for this important step belongs to my loyal wife and her sister, May. It was entirely through their influence and perseverance that this first phase of healing took place.

"Looking back on those days of extremity in what now seems another lifetime, I discern ever more clearly the intricate and wondrous workings of God through circumstances and through those trying to help me. After the treatment I temporarily lost my craving for alcohol. However, the doctors warned me that the desire would begin to return within a few weeks. Their advice was that, in the intervening period of abstinence, I should build up physical and mental strength to fight the insistent craving when it returned. During this time, in early September, the full realization of my plight came to me with shocking force. Amidst growing anxiety, I knew that I must find help outside of myself. Self-will alone was not strong enough to win the uneven contest.

"Dread of what lay ahead was filling me with dismay. In desperation one afternoon I picked up and began to read a book called *I Was A Pagan* by V. C. Kitchen. Wisely never referring to it, my wife had left the book lying conspicuously on a table for several months. Unquestionably, my impulse to read this book was an answer to prayer, and I emphasize here the important fact that Wilda and her new friends had been praying for me for many weeks. Never shall I be able to express all the gratitude I feel toward the dedicated, believing souls who faithfully prayed for my healing in those dark days. My wife somehow had known that real help could come to me through *I Was A Pagan*. Now that it was necessary that she be in Washington for two months, I was alone trying to win my crucial battle, and the book she had hoped I would read became an important factor in future developments. With compelling, excited eagerness I read page after page and went on to the end. For the first time I learned and believed that God cares so deeply for each one of His children that He yearns to help each of us in any difficulty whatsoever, excessive drinking included. Never before had I understood this wondrous truth; in fact, I had mistakenly assumed that God would not bother about such a weakness as over-indulgence in alcohol. Now my thinking was revolutionized and new hope was born.

"Immediately following my first reading of this book, I began to pray everyday, asking God for help and strength to overcome the desire for drink. On my knees praying at least five or six times a day occupied many hours, and each day of prayer seemed to make me stronger and to increase my courage. Resolve strengthened in me and, with God's help, I determined to cure permanently the disease which was destroying my life.

"About ten days after reading the book, what I had been dreading happened, the torturing desire for drink returned. However, now I had a new and powerful source of strength, a new and powerful ally. My fervent praying continued for the next three weeks as I fought to the utmost to resist temptation. I knew there was only one way to total victory, I must learn to face intoxicants without fear. Therefore, Wilda and I had agreed to leave our liquor in its customary place. Otherwise, how could I ever be really triumphant?

"One day at twilight, I was pacing our living room in a tense manner. Filled with abject fear that I would succumb to the temptation which seemed close to overpowering me, I had never before felt as desperate or as lost. My struggle not to be overcome, not to reach for a drink, was being waged so fiercely that large drops of perspiration were drenching my forehead. Nevertheless, my invisible enemy appeared to be shattering my defenses. Throwing myself on my knees, I prayed with genuine abandon and with all the intensity brought on by my appalling need.

"I do not know how long I had been kneeling before a sudden, mysterious sense of a presence in the room caused me to lift my head in bewilderment. By now darkness was near, but I had turned on no lamps. Therefore, I was astounded to see a strong white light shining in the far corner of the room. I seemed to be immersed in a hushed and expectant moment of breathlessness, and my perplexed mind at first thought that I must be dying. At the next instant I experienced a sensation of overwhelming peace and joy, and my body began to glow and tingle with an unearthly sense of well-being.

"At this point, my whole self became aware that the vision was of divine origin. Then came the realization that a figure stood in the light, a figure larger than life-size, covering the entire corner wall up to the ceiling. With blinding revelation the knowledge filled me that the Risen Christ was standing before me. Tremblingly, I lost myself in the beauty of this vision. My eyes were slowly and irresistibly drawn to those of the Saviour. A terrific impact of pure love utterly transcending any life experience pulsated through me in waves of rapture.

"I also saw in His eyes an indescribable softness, a humanly unimaginable warmth and glow. In familiar terms, but magnified countlessly, looking into His eyes was almost like rediscovering an old friend. A thrill of joyous recognition surged within me, as I felt His response to my acute awareness of our eternal relationship. I knew from His face and expression, and wordlessly He told me, that I was no longer on my own. He would always sustain me. Unutterable joy flooded me as I realized that our Saviour had come to me personally. By His power I was reborn.

"Hopelessly inadequate to portray the invasion of the natural by the supernatural are all words of this world. Ineffable beauty and man's bliss from contact with the Divine are, by their very truth, humanly indescribable. They are also utterly staggering to the human senses. After the brief moment of glorious reality in which I met Jesus face to face, I remained as if in a trance or as if lifted up into another world. On my knees for at least half an hour longer, almost overcome with ecstasy, I poured out gratitude and rejoicing to the Father for this greatest of blessings which had been given to me and for the indefinable but sure sense of victory over my weakness. It is hard to recall anything else about that evening except that I finally went to bed, still feeling in a state of other-worldly suspension.

"In the middle of the night I was awakened by what seemed to be a voice speaking to me. 'You must get up and go to the kitchen cabinet to look at the liquor bottles.' Believing the voice a vagary of a dream or some other illusion, I tried to go back to sleep and to ignore the words, but they were repeated insistently. Now fully awake, I was amazed. During the foregoing period of temptation, I had not even dared see those bottles for fear I would drink from them. Now all my fear had left me, even though the strange compulsion to go to the liquor cabinet continued. Not really knowing why and not at all understanding my own actions, I reluctantly arose and went to look at the bottles containing the same liquid which had been my undoing many times. Gazing upon that which a few hours earlier had been so agonizingly tempting, everything now was changed. The bottles evoked in me no emotion whatsoever; for all the effect they had on me, they might as well have held ink instead of whiskey. At that instant, I knew in unmistakable fashion that drinking would never again be a problem in my life. God had completely and permanently removed from my mind and body all craving and all need for alcohol.

"For over twenty-five years now the life-changing results

of that September night have given peace and happiness to myself and to my wife. I would like to point out that in all these years I have never had to use will power not to drink. God-Power has utterly blotted out the temptation. In the twinkling of an eye, I became thoroughly dispassionate about liquor and, no matter how much I have come in contact with it, never again has it held any appeal for me. To my mind, this fact emphasizes one of the most glorious truths about our loving Father. Even as His generosity and His love are beyond human comprehension, so His answers to prayer far outreach our limited asking. In my finiteness, I had been praying for help and strength to fight a self-destructive desire. In His infinity, God not only gave me help and strength but also eliminated the desire itself. God alone with His illimitable supremacy can and does accomplish such miracles. 'And now unto Him who is able to do exceeding abundantly above all that we ask or think, according to the power that worketh in us.' "

6

INITIATION

The night before the next message I had a vivid dream. Lowell and I were in school together. This seemed entirely natural because the class was composed of both children and adults. I dreamed Lowell was having an important examination, and, to my great happiness, he passed the test. In my dream, I realized how much this meant and that it was a milestone in his growth, also a kind of initiation into a higher realm.

Two other remarks of Lowell's in this message may be of special interest. The first is his saying that finances would no longer be an ever-present problem in our life. Such has been the case. After many years of strained financial affairs, with our new way of living came an almost unconscious release from troublesome burdens and worries that had always plagued us. Unimportant values and ways of living began to drop away, even budgets and expenses seemed to fall into place, into their useful and rightful, but less glaringly prominent place.

Lowell's second remark I would mention is the one in reference to a coming crisis. He speaks of the "active" part his father will play in spite of the fact that Franklin was then retired from active duty in the Navy and in ill health. Nevertheless, his health became much improved and, in 1939, he was recalled to duty and continued to serve all through the Second World War. The "indirect" part I was to play must refer to my Gray Lady and other war work of that type. As Lowell says, his own contributions were "unseen," but I am sure he was often with me, in fact often guiding me, in my many contacts with young servicemen during those war-filled years. Without question, his "unseen part" was of larger scope than that because we know that in his present existence he lives only to serve and that he can do so in much less limited form than any of us here on earth.

Coronado, California
December 26, 1937

"I am coming—coming through to you. Don't be afraid, Mom. I am here. You know I am close to you, so why do you feel sad?

"I am on earth-work for the first time in many weeks and am sending out some of the impulses I have been learning. I have passed my first examinations, that is why you dreamed you were trying to help me in my studies last night. Yes, there are old and young spirits all together in school just as you dreamed. We have no age here. All work toward ultimate perfection, and age means only stages of development. I have learned much. You know how little I knew. Even the things I learned from you and Dad, Sunday School, Boy Scouts and Alice Deal School—all these are only a trifle compared to what I learn in a day here.

"A day is not a day as you know it, but a segregation of spiritual illumination. I have reached a higher plane in a very short time, and you and Dad are keeping right up with me since his healing. You are now on a higher plane in a new life. We will always go on together. We are an intimate circle, a ray of the same light beam working by magnetism, like one tone of music or one atom of matter.

I know all your energies and your moods, they all take the form of thought waves.

"Don't wonder anymore about how I will look when you see me. It isn't like that, Mom, it is nicer. Oh! gee, I can't seem to make you understand. You will know me. I am still Lowell, Lowell, Lowell, only more! I was just a body plus a mind to develop and a spirit. Now I am spirit plus a mind to develop and a curious body, not shapeful or concrete, but conscious of itself and able to navigate through space like smoke. I can see myself like a light, you can see and feel me only with your intuition.

"You and Dad are happier now and will have greater happiness as you climb the ladder of spiritual accomplishment. Worry no more about money. That will no longer be a serious problem.

"Perhaps sometime I will be allowed to talk directly to you, but now it must be indirectly, through impulses. You are not 'queer' Mom. You have perceptive vision and through this gift you will make others see and feel. Great conflicts are indeed coming. This battle between good and evil will come to a real crisis soon. Dad has an active part to play, you an indirect one and I an unseen part. It matters not how great or small our parts, for we are one, now and for always.

"I have to go now but I will come again."

Lowell's happiness about his father's healing which had taken place three months earlier is obvious. A thrilling example of spiritual rebirth and the absolute power of Christ's love, in this one moment of divine contact, Franklin's relationship with God was rectified. Jesus Christ came to him in healing glory and power to release him and to give him newness of life. Naturally, a period of gradual spiritual development and of adjustment to his new life followed. After finding himself healed from the terrible disease of alcoholism, his next step was proper orientation to his new self. Then he built up new relationships with family and friends which, in turn, became preparation for his future. With God's patient, understanding love and assistance, the prophecy came true, "If any man be in Christ, he is a new creature; old things are passed away; behold, all things are become new." In an earlier message Lowell says of his father, "When he asks and believes more fully," and Franklin's reward for doing so was more glorious and complete than any of us could have imagined.

With all my heart I rejoice that we are now living in an age of clearer realization of the problem of alcoholism; new therapeutic measures have also been discovered. No longer treated as an outcast, the alcoholic is recognized as a seriously sick patient, but always as one with very real hope for recovery. The Great Physician will provide healing, but there is one absolute requirement on the patient's part. He must honestly want to stop drinking. God will not be mocked or deluded. Having given each of us free will, our Heavenly Father must wait until we make our own decision and ask. "Ask and ye shall receive."

7

AT THE COMMUNION RAIL

In early February we were at the altar of our church receiving communion. Suddenly I was so flooded with the feeling of Lowell's presence at the communion rail with us that I was left with a sharp desire for the earthly Lowell. I yearned to touch him, to see again his laughing brown eyes, his mischievous smile and his sturdy body. I wanted my son back with me in the flesh and, for the moment, I could accept nothing else. Knowing I could not have Lowell here on earth with me, an acute return of my old enemy, longing for death to join Lowell, swept over me. After leaving the church, the relief of tears helped restore me. But it was the following message, written almost immediately afterwards, which gave me peace and joy again and urged me on to a more complete surrender of the physical Lowell.

I tell of this incident to point out that, despite my contacts with the invisible world, I was often still all-too-human in my reactions, in my loneliness and nostalgia. The above happens to have been a particularly poignant episode for me, but all growth has its painful struggles and setbacks. Throughout this book will be discovered many fluctuations of mood and temperament on my part, many ups and downs of emotional and spiritual life, and many "dry" periods in contrast to the more fertile ones. We were learning that spiritual life and development are beset with doubt and failure. Yet the rewards are infinitely rich. The larger picture is the one that counts, and, given the perspective of later years, we can all recognize important landmarks in our own growth. This was one such day for me. Lowell, himself, said this Sunday, "You and Dad are just starting on the work you are meant to do." The truth of his statement is easy to see now. Franklin and I were beginning to learn to pray together, and we were working to straighten out troublesome details in our relationship to each other. We were frequently participating in prayer fellowship with the group I had met last summer. Thus, we were being helped to develop spiritually, to reorient our personalities and to express our very real gratitude to God by giving ourselves in service to others. His healing of Franklin and His guiding Hand in our more complete release of Lowell were leading us to a happiness and joy in our marriage such as we had never known before. In addition, I was conscious of Lowell's soul-development and my own need and yearning to keep up with him. All these factors made more intense our longing to commit every area of our lives to God.

Coronado, California
February 6, 1938

"Mom, I am sorry that my coming upset you. I wanted you to know that our spirits are close. I came to tell you that I can understand your thoughts better all the time. You had a shiny light around your hair; I saw it around Daddy, too, when I looked into your vibrations. I went to see what it was, and your prayers, so beautiful at the altar, were like music coming up from the light. So I came to bless you and Daddy and to let you know everything is all right. Never have things been better.

"Mom, you still think I need you, but all I need is your love and your prayers. As you and Dad give yourselves to spiritual things, you are giving love to me, for I am spirit,

just a tiny part of God's light and truth. I am still Lowell, but clothed in a new raiment—not in the old, brown suit which went into flames in the crematory. I am not in any suit. I am just pure love which touched your heart during the communion service and aroused your mother-love for the old me. Mom, you can't come here yet. It would spoil everything. You and Dad are just starting on the work you are meant to do. I am here to steer you straight when you get a little off course. I am the closest bond you have, the symbol of love and devotion. However, I am only a small part of the great love and devotion of God. Why should you want me, when the whole supply is ready for you to take? You have not lost me—you have me and, through memory of me, you shall be led to reach out for greater gifts.

"Your earthly happiness is just a sample of what your spiritual happiness will be when you completely surrender the physical me. My passing was a gateway and an escape. I was not hurt by it, nor bewildered for long; I was re-charged with greater vitality, like a battery fully charged for the first time and useful at last."

8

SHOOTING DUCKS

Despite all the blessings of the past year, despite new insight, I again somewhat dreaded Lowell's birthday. I again allowed myself to become momentarily upset by my maternal longings. Nevertheless, I realized that Lowell was speaking the truth when he said that his father and I were progressing toward greater happiness than ever before. We were not only beginning to know the meaning of spiritual joy in our life and marriage, but we were also discovering for ourselves that the "selfless service" he speaks of draws one closer to God. The nearer to God, the nearer to our son we became, and we rejoiced because we were working with our boy and assisting him in strengthening the quality of his ongoingness. Correspondingly, every richer contact with Lowell increased our awareness of the One we three were earnestly seeking to serve, individually and together as a unit of love. Lowell's reference here to fun and duck-shooting delighted me. He was still our little boy, he still remembered! Lowell had loved to go duck hunting with his father; in fact, like his father, he was an excellent shot. Some of Franklin's happiest memories of his son are of their early morning hunting expeditions. They often went to Chesapeake Bay together and, my husband remembers, when the weather was so bitterly cold that he and his friends would give up, Lowell, with his youthful zest and unmindfulness of the elements, would continue to shoot.

Once, when Lowell was only thirteen, he and his father

were invited by the Commandant of the Naval Station to shoot in his blind on the Potomac. The two men would stand and shoot first, then would come Lowell's opportunity. Franklin well remembers his own embarrassment when, several different times, his son skillfully brought down a bird which the Commandant had just missed.

I was overjoyed to learn that Lowell was having more fun now than shooting ducks!

Coronado, California
May 14, 1938

"Mom, today power is coming through smoothly. Are you not rejoicing that I can speak to you and, through you, to others?

"I am seventeen, yes, in your way of thinking, but there is no time here nor standard of measurement. I am still Lowell, surrounded by love and friends, adventure and happiness. Lately you have seemed more aware of how close I am to you in spirit, so why let memories of little physical details or mere dates on the calendar upset your balance?

"You will be happier this year than ever before. You and Daddy will have more of the happiness I am having. I am encircling you continually, but your mortal imagination believes me nearer at times like this. I thought you would like to feel me more consciously because I knew the wound of my passing was healing. However, I will try not to force things and will wait until you invite me.

"Mom, you are attuned to positive currents, you are like a radio set. You can tune in whatever you like whenever you are quiet and receptive. You can contact me when you need me. The static which causes confusion between us is

caused by doubts, fears and too many questions asking for proof.

"From your world today, a layer of mist is rising which clouds the two worlds. Rays of light which come from faith and love can penetrate through the mist or through any evil thing, eternally and continually. These rays are the only lasting power which can rise from the earth through to the harmony of our world.

"Send love to me when you want my response, love and prayer for my unfolding. I really am growing now, and I can understand more clearly. When you and Dad progress and help clear up the earth fog by selfless service, you are making closer contact with me and also causing our influences to penetrate better. We cannot transmit when hatred blocks the way. We cannot enter the consciousness of those who willfully cut themselves off from good. We can enter minds and hearts which are turned to God, or which have even a tiny desire-crack for good. You haven't any idea of the power coming through, it is more each day. The work you are doing is hastening this perfect contact. The desire, just the desire, to reach out to help lets us in.

"I am working with boys. When they are asleep and unaware, I shoot a love-beam into them and make them want good. Evil, too, always waits for its opening to get ahead of us. We have to watch for a little crack to shoot in the power of good. It is fun, Mom! It is more fun than shooting ducks. Each boy or girl, man or woman, who turns to God and higher things is increasing our influence. Do try, all of you, to make people know that power is available, if you but ask. When you doubt, we lose a bit of ground; when you accept power, more power is released. I can work with Daddy better all the time. I can work best through your love for me but, when you doubt, even that love is not enough."

9

THE SLOW ASCENT

In September of 1938 we returned to Washington to re-rent our home there. To go back where we three had lived together created an emotional challenge. Finding the house, in which Lowell had lived so zestfully and happily, left in poor condition by its tenants added a discouraging note. Furthermore, one of my problems has always been the confusion which threatens to disrupt me when I am in a crowded city. I seem to be unusually sensitive to the thoughts and moods of others and the cross-vibrations of many people tend to disturb me. Having become accustomed to life in a small town, I was attempting to readjust myself to the tempo of a large and busy city. Lowell, therefore, in this message is trying to encourage me and to help me through a rather difficult time.

The dream he mentions had affected me deeply, and I still recall it very clearly after all these years. It was as if I saw the whole human race marching up a hill toward a great light. Countless figures were in the procession, each one different from the others in some way. Many dark figures plodded wearily along with heads lowered and eyes on the ground. There were those who were stooped and lame, but some, even in this group, walked buoyantly. In the endless parade, I could also distinguish faces radiantly alight and joy-filled. Whatever I glimpsed in the various separate marchers was fascinating, but the point of the dream seemed to be the hill itself. Its slope was gradual, and all the human race was on it. Always the slow ascent, always upward toward the Light advanced the climb of evolution.

Washington, D. C.
September 15, 1938

"I am your shadow, not a dark shadow but the light part of you. I shine like reflected sun, and I inject my reflection into your mind. I can come into your thoughts because I can go anywhere, and you need more light to make you think more clearly. There are so many destructive vibrations around the earth that they are crowding everywhere, inside and outside people. There are more in crowds than in quiet places; that is why you like the beauty of the mountains, the sea and open spaces. I can help to ward off evil from you and Dad in the same way that you protected me when I was a little boy.

"I am on a great journey, Mom, just as you dreamed last night, and some day you will be with me. Everyone who has love and faith in God's power will be together in one element. People think more here. We don't have bodies to care for, but we do have great thought power. We are using it to direct all good forces to work together so that evil cannot permeate people's minds and actions. I am glad you have released me. However, I still need your love and prayers to help me in the big conflict.

"This is a letter to you just like one I would write if I were on a trip somewhere. I am well and happy and I have much to tell you and Dad. I know what you are doing, you know in your hearts what I am doing. Even though you cannot see me with your eyes, you can see and feel me with your spirit. I am all spirit, I can pass through anything.

You could not lock me out with steel or stone, for I can travel instantly like a light ray or a thought.

"I have to study a great deal, but it is fun because we see instantly why we learn things. We acquire knowledge and then use it right away. On earth you are slower. You often learn a good thing only to bury it away and forget it, perhaps for years. Here, older spirits answer our questions, and immediately we experiment with the knowledge gained.

"The mind is more vital than the body, it is brighter and eternal. Most human minds, however, are too active or too swirling-around for us to enter. When a mind is quiet, it becomes clear or more receptive. I am much more alive than you realize. I am the real Lowell now."

10

THE ETERNAL URGE

During this period, I read several books on immortality. A friend loaned me *Horizons of Eternity* by Palmstierna. While reading it, I felt a strong urge to write. The few paragraphs which follow are the result. I am including them because they seem to fit in well with Lowell's thoughts written a few weeks earlier. From time to time in this book, when they seem suitable, I intend to include a few thoughts from many writings which came to me rapidly, intuitively and in the same manner as those from Lowell. It may be interesting to observe the difference in the style of writing.

Washington, D. C.
October 1, 1938

"God has a plan for each and every soul. That plan is elastic, adjustable and sensitive to eventuality. It embraces all stages of progress—the prenatal, earth's material existence, the transformation to spirit again at death and the clarification to purer intensity of light as souls move nearer perfection. God or perfection is the indescribable, vibrant mass of dazzling spiritual intelligence which is symbolized as pure light or truth.

"As you draw away from the perfect light, you enter shadows and darkness. Evil possesses you. Then you must suffer and become victims of abnormal circumstance until the urge of the irresistible magnet of light and power draws you back.

"*Some take years or lifetimes and must suffer agony and death before they start their journey back. Others (spiritual souls) get their balance quickly and do not lose momentum. Therefore, it matters not what your previous existence was if, in your present state of consciousness, you are tingling with the eternal urge to find your way toward the light. Your desire forms the current back to the Divine Mind.*"

11

THE LIGHTED CROSS

To progress to the short writing of May first, I would speak briefly of the dream to which it refers. Incidentally, I often dream vividly of Lowell the night before a message from him is to come to me. On the night of April thirtieth, I saw another procession of marching figures, but this time Lowell was its leader. Immediately I was reminded of his choirboy experience while on earth. Lowell, who had possessed a lovely boy-soprano voice, sang in our choir for years. There appeared to be an analogy between that fact and the dream, perhaps because he was now carrying a beautiful cross all aglow with light. Lowell himself was radiant with joy, and I saw him as an exalted spirit who had just won a victory. As I became aware that he had taken another victorious step, I knew more convincingly than ever that all was well with my son. On awakening, I discovered that Lowell's emotions had communicated themselves to me. An extraordinary sense of well-being, a feeling of great peace and an intensity of joy filled me. Intuitively I knew that not only had Lowell advanced in the realm of spirit but that his father and I were receiving new understanding through his influence. Exactly as in my dream procession, Lowell from that day on was to be the leader while his earthly parents were to follow rejoicing.

Coronado, California
May 1, 1939

"I am tuning in to you and Dad this morning. You are

not holding me back now and are, therefore, helping me in the fight against evil. God is releasing power all the time. He does not supply it more rapidly because you on earth could not receive it. You are not yet equipped with enough spiritual capacity to accept its full inflow. This force is greater by far than any on earth. It is really vital. It is what makes life and light. Only as man asks can it be released, atom by atom. You must help men to ask for this power and to want God above all else.

"I am now the opening wedge of a youth movement. I lead invisibly, I am carrying the cross of which you dreamed. I am pulsating with currents of vital life, as you sensed in your dream. You well know in your heart that this faith of ours is indestructible.

"Dad is doing wonderfully, and I am very proud of him. Your heart is warm today. I feel it and it helps me here."

12

TESTING TIME

More than a year elapsed before the next message. 1939 and 1940 were years of great tension and crucial world problems; the Second World War was beginning and the news was grim and foreboding. Our personal lives had also experienced suffering and discouragement. My husband had been seriously ill this year and I, too, was having times of physical limitation. Our energy was depleted, and we certainly needed the advice Lowell gives us here as well as his every assistance in reaching the "new heights" to which he refers.

Lowell tells how our doctor-friend from the other side is helping me to attain better health. This reminds me of an episode during Franklin's illness. In February he had to undergo extremely serious surgery. I waited out the operation at the surgeon's home with members of my family. I seemed almost to feel the knife and the pain within myself. Seeking to be alone to pray, I went upstairs and knelt in solitude and silence before the Lord. As if in answer, three short but revivifying sentences from Lowell came to me clearly.

"Mom, there is nothing to fear. The best doctors on this side are guiding the surgeon's knife. Dad will be all right."

I walked downstairs with peace instead of turmoil within me. Feeling convinced that all was well, I became so relaxed that I actually fell asleep on a couch in a room full of people. Within five minutes the phone woke me with the finest possible news from Franklin's doctor. He said the crisis was over and the operation a full success. His "Franklin will be all right" sang in my heart with Lowell's identical words of a few minutes earlier. Together these merged into a joyous melody of praise to the Giver of all life.

Long Beach, California
June 5, 1940

"Mom, don't be so serious. Look at the sky and know that I am there and in the wind and the sea. I am everywhere, although it is difficult to reach you if your thoughts are indwelling. I long to lure you to new heights, but your lack of energy is retarding you. Forget all that and soar with me. Let your real self, your spirit self, dominate. Tread on air, laugh, Mom. Laughter releases your spirit which is cooped up in your body. I cannot breathe without freedom, and I could not live in my old body and be happy like this.

"I am so busy that I cannot remember all the earth things the way I did at first. They fade like baby thoughts. We are not 'up' or 'far away' but right near you in the magnetic sphere of thought and love. When you send love waves to me I respond. When you have a negative vibration I lose my clear contact with you. If we are to connect and communicate, we must learn how to synchronize our thought-waves. Joy, love and all spiritual qualities weld our spirits together.

"The world will be saved. We are winning the invisible battle first. You must not be a wavering beacon of light but must be a steadfast one. Please do not ever say again that you and Dad are getting old and useless. Never say a thing like that unless you want it to be true. Know and believe that your spirits are alive like mine. Spirit is all that really counts. Bodies merely contain spirit. God does not look at

the body but at the life inside. He accepts your desires and efforts, not your failures and drawbacks. More affirmations will buoy you up. Say, 'I am eternally alive, radiant, joyful and released in God's limitless energy and love.' Live and breathe in the oceans of energy all around you.

"Dr. George* is here, and he is helping you. I am sending you impulses and healing currents relayed from him.

"Dad needs to play and laugh more. World conditions have discouraged him. His emotions go out to suffering and strained affairs but not often enough to God's energy. Oh, I wish I could say it the right way—I am here with you now, and I want to help you. I sing as I work. Can you not feel it? Sometimes I try to sing into your hearts, but other things distract you. Please let me in more often."

---

* See Preface.

13

ECHOES OF JOY

The next day, Lowell was still urging me on to "new heights" of joy and laughter and dancing hearts. I well remember our one real dance together, to which he refers. While we were in Maine that last summer, we went to a community country-dance, I wearing a gay red dress and inappropriate high-heeled shoes. A hardy lobster fisherman became my partner for a square dance. He was swinging and flinging me around in wholehearted enthusiasm, but my high heels were making this kind of dancing too perilous for pleasure. I certainly needed rescuing from my strenuous partner, and who should laughingly observe my plight but Lowell. Gallantly, he cut in, remarking that my predicament was my own fault for wearing a bright red dress.

No one but a mother can understand the unique thrill which comes from dancing with her son. This was our first and only dance, but its joy remains with me. Lowell was his most adult self, charmingly attentive and full of joy and laughter. I stress the joy and laughter because Lowell's comparison between eternal joy and laughter and the emotions we shared during that summer's dance is apt indeed. I am keenly aware that what I felt in those moments was, at the very least, an echo of eternal joy. Amazingly similar have been my moments of other-worldly exaltation and ecstasy. Laughter is a key. Abundant joy is the revelation. Lowell's spirit is full of both, and he is trying hard to make me more capable of absorbing and sharing these emotions.

Long Beach, California
June 6, 1940

"Try to be happier, Mom. Let your spirit swing to eternal rhythm. Remember how we danced on earth? I danced then with my body. Now I really dance in true motion, joy and momentum. You know how it is when you are tingling with life and feel you cannot keep your feet on the ground where they belong? That is something the way I feel here, continually charged and recharged with energy and joy. Mom, God is Life. That means a power of which you cannot conceive. Even here we cannot take too much God-Power. It would stun and retard us. However, as we progress, we can take more and more.

"I try to send life rays to you and Dad, although you are not always receptive. I can penetrate some minds, often more easily when people are asleep. At that time, their negative thoughts and self-wills are not blocking the way.

"Please help me in my experiments. I will not overdo them and make you unhappy as I did a year ago at the Communion Service when I was less experienced. I was cautioned about my mistakes, but my teachers are fine and are letting me find out for myself where I can be most useful. I like to go where there is laughter, not where there are sad, serious thoughts. When you laugh, I am there. It does not have to be out loud—just laugh in your heart."

14

ADVENTURE IN SALESMANSHIP

Again I was in Washington, this time alone and in an attempt to sell our home there. By this time I had learned the folly of taking any important step unless it were based on prayer. Ideally, the spiritual should be an accepted and integral part of every business transaction, of every relationship, of every undertaking of any kind and, of course, I prayed for guidance about selling the house. In addition, I tried to do what Lowell suggests in the next message, to picture the house filled with only our happiest memories. Prayerfully I asked that the right buyers be led to it.

Among others, a young couple with several children appeared interested in the house. They kept coming back to see it, regardless of the fact that they did not at first think they should spend as much money as was involved. Finally their sincerity and genuine reluctance to give up the house made me feel that they were the ones who should have it. Therefore, and I have always been glad I did so, I decided to sell to them with a considerably smaller down payment than planned. I knew Lowell's boyhood home would be in good hands and that other children would now build new and happy memories into permanency there.

There is a law of demand and supply. There is a law— "Give and ye shall receive." This adventure in selling taught me a simple rule of successful salesmanship. In thinking equally of the needs of the buyer and the seller, the two-way need will be met and both will benefit. Incidentally, we have used this technique successfully many times in renting our California home—just one more proof that Christ's way works in business as well as in all other phases of life.

Junie is mentioned once again in this message. He had been graduated from high school in June of this year. Having reached a time for decision, in common with many young men in 1940, he was unsettled in his mind and uncertain of his future. Consequently, we asked him to come to Coronado to live with us for a while. He accepted our invitation and was with us for several months. Junie fitted into our life beautifully and seemed more than ever like a son to us. I am sure his being with us pleased Lowell and I remember that we often were aware of Lowell's joyous influence in those months. During this time, Junie took some postgraduate classes in our high school and gradually his plans began to evolve. Having found his sense of direction, he joined the Naval Reserve and was ordered to active duty on a naval transport. This, in turn, led to his entering Annapolis, where he graduated with high honors in 1946.

Washington, D. C.
August 10, 1940

"Mom is my code word. Do you hear me? I try to say things, but you sometimes still think you imagine me.

"What an adventure you could have selling the house! I will tell you about it. You caught some of the idea yesterday. Earth experiences become permanent memories only when they are clothed in spiritual traits and emotions. The happiness we had in that house is a permanent picture building toward a crystalization of perfection. The unhappiness simply fades out of the picture. Like the bright colors of an oil painting, loyalty, unselfishness and all good quali-

ties help make the beautiful lasting part. When one says or does an unworthy thing, it is as if one blurred or blotted out the beauty, thus making the picture messy and ugly. So it is with every thought in your life. Thoughts make the urge to act and actions make the character or spiritual picture.

"When you go to the house today, ask for every happy memory connected with it to stand out and all the rest to fade. In this way you will fill the house with joy and light. It will then call out to the susceptible souls who want such a house. Speak for the house, asking those to come to it who need such a haven. They will feel the call and be drawn as if by a magnet. Believe me, this is an adventure in vibration. You can do anything and everything by sending out calls. Your heart and mind are broadcasting stations more powerful than man-made ones. Therefore, fill your house with spiritual magnetism and know that happy results will follow.

"I am helping Junie, and he is really waking up. I am sending him powerful impulses which are the leaven of development. He is just beginning his climb and has a bright pathway ahead. Love is the motivating force of all good impulses. If you love enough, you, too, can be a living current to pass on these impulses. If you hate or become small with self-centeredness, you are giving control to vagrant impulses.

"Mike is stunned. Pray for him to be able to feel again. He has not yet awakened but I am watching over him. I tried to warn you about him. He could not understand the meaning of life, and he still cannot see it. He will sleep and someday enough love will awaken him."

An explanation is required concerning Mike who was a close friend of Franklin's. Even before my train reached the Washington station that August day, I felt an unaccountable impulse to telephone Mike. In fact, it is not exaggeration to say that I felt commanded to do so. Three times I was inwardly told that I must call him. Yet, I disregarded those strong intuitive urges; rather, I resisted them and tried not to listen. My rationalizing was understandable from a worldly point of view. I was just finishing a long cross-country train trip, and Mike was not as close a friend of mine as of my husband. Frankly, I thought it was a rather peculiar and almost improper time to call him. Certainly, to wait a few days would be more sensible, I reasoned.

Such regret, such deep pangs of remorse as I experienced on learning the next day of Mike's suicide a few hours after my arrival. Too late I realized that Lowell, who had been very fond of Mike, had tried persistently to obtain my help. Mike had loved him, too, and a real bond had existed between them. As a boy, Lowell had been fascinated by planes, and Mike was one of the Army's top aviators. The older man delighted Lowell with his stories of aviation and often gave him presents. An autographed Lindbergh photograph, I remember, was one which Lowell especially treasured. Easily reconstructed is the picture of a boy's idealized love for a hero and the affection of the man for the enthusiastic, responsive youth. The point to stress, though, is that once again we see that love does not die, that it continues to live and grow after death. In this one message we have concrete evidence of that fact and of its importance in our lives, even when we are entirely unaware of it. Lowell and his mother, Lowell and Junie, Lowell and Mike, this world and the next world, linked inseparably together by the most powerful force in existence—love.

For my part, I shall never forget what I learned from this experience concerning Mike. Outlined with tragedy, the lesson left an indelible impression. It taught me to respect any persistent inner urge and to obey even when I cannot find reasons for the impulse. In the guided life, I believe implicitly that unseen friends and loved ones often try to lead us to help ourselves and, more significantly, others in need. I pray that never again may I fail them the way I did on that day of my arrival in Washington.

15

LOVE, LIFT AND LAUGH

"Love, lift and laugh" is the theme of the message which came on Lowell's twentieth birthday. It is a recurring theme running through the entire book, as will be noted. Surely, no one will question the value of "love, lift and laugh" for even the darkest times. May 1941 looked decidedly black for this world. Nevertheless, most of the time I almost guiltily clung to a strange sense of joy. Despite grim head-lines and tragic events, God was still in control, the rampant terror was temporary terror. Of course, I was often tempted to become disheartened by bad news. Similarly, in matters of health it is difficult not to falter in faith when unfavorable symptoms arise. During these days of world crisis, however, Lowell's influence and his longer-range vision were at least partly responsible for the joy I often experienced.

Coronado, California
May 15, 1941

"Mom, today I am twenty in your years but only an infant in real time. Why is time so important to man? There is no time in eternity, no beginning, no end. Time is meas-ured in stages of light and love. Each age of man on earth leaves an imprint on eternity's chart. When masses of man-kind reach out in love and faith, the indicator reaches a new level. Although at present the earth looks dark to you, the indicator has reached an all time high. Can you not

see that man is afraid, confused and desperate because he realizes that his mind and will have brought only chaos to the world? Now he must reach out toward the only infallible light—love, a love bigger than himself.

"Men on earth long for the God of love. Therefore, praise Him that more and more souls are choosing His way. You are right not to let war news or people's hopeless thoughts and words pull you down. Reach out to God, and He will lift you up even as Christ lifted up draws all men towards Himself.

"Your physical condition is only a shadow. Never have you and Dad been better. Do not heed physical limitations; ignore them. However, be sensible and obey nature's laws so that you can better understand and use spiritual laws. We are governed here entirely by spirit regulations.

"I wish I could remove your negative trait of clinging to the past. Believe in the invisible present and the glorious future. Believe in the finished story. You could not yet comprehend the majesty of the real story of the human soul, and neither could I find words to tell you!

"I heard your prayer this morning and saw a radiant light about you. Remember that higher souls here are working with no letup to change the tide of humanity toward good. People do strange, impulsive things today and usually do not understand that we on this side are influencing them. When we see an opening for good, we inject love; however, evil is also injecting itself at every opportunity. We are having to work hard, for all souls who come here with war and race hatred in their consciousness have a deterring effect on our plans.

"Today I shall hover near to let you know that I am still your boy, yet now a man and growing into my eternal ego. I was a drifter at first when I could not take anything

seriously enough. Gradually I was taught my purpose, and now I live only to fulfill that. We are born on earth to learn lessons to use here. Earthly love is a mere shadow of love expressed on this plane. Even our love here is only a feeble ray compared to the love Christ offers to man. Why cannot man accept it and use it? Then all would be well. Stubborn, blind, selfish man! Only through these black, and ever blacker approaching clouds will he learn his lesson.

"The true light, God's Light of Love, will never go out. All men shall be drawn toward it and finally swallowed up in it. There shall be no darkness nor night, but when or how that time will come no one knows. As we obey orders and walk silently, joyfully in the direction of that light, we are encouraged, instructed and loved by higher souls.

"Enjoy earth's beauties and love its purposes, too, for in the twinkling of an eye, earth shall become a shadowy memory. But love, laughter and joy go on forever. Drink deeply of these, and they will be the means of guiding you into the life here.

"Your new home is beautiful, and its light shines out across the island. Do not let anything put out that light. Only light, love and faith can swallow up the blackness of night. Prayer and desire, the twin candles, are keeping the inner lights burning. Your thoughts and love drew me to you. I am with you because light and love are there."

Our life continued to be extremely busy, even though we still had personal problems with which to contend. The Navy had been on a wartime basis for some time and Franklin was spending long hours at his work. I was active in church and other outside work in addition to running the large new house mentioned above.

We tried always to keep our new home alight with love,

as Lowell had urged. The house had also been planned and
built with prayer very much a part of the whole undertaking. We had prayed everyday for the workmen and for
their personal needs; we prayed that the house would be
beautiful in God's sight and useful in His service. We
thanked Him for the privilege of building this home and,
of course, we asked for His help and guidance in its actual
construction, with the result that construction headaches
were at a minimum and even the knottiest problems more
simply solved. Our dear friend, Bishop Harris, led a dedication service when the house was completed. As joyous as
this moment was, we little realized its full significance and
the wealth of experience which was to be ours in our new
home.

For nine busy years we lived there, and abundant evidence was given to us of the rewards of dedicating a home
to God. We can testify that He does take over and use a
home when invited. In this case, we were part of a vital
prayer fellowship for which our home was used many times.
I often wonder how we ourselves could have gone through
those difficult war years without the understanding fellowship we knew in that home. In addition, other lives were
changed and healed through the power of God's love. As
always, He did the works, not we ourselves. Sometimes our
house seemed almost like a clinic, and one of the happiest
results was that often those who had come seeking help
eventually became a source of help to others. So does the
Kingdom grow. One prayer group directly or indirectly
causes others to be initiated. One home dedicated to God
inspires others to invite Christ to take over their homes. Indeed, none of us can estimate the results to our world of
even one Christ-filled life.

When Christ has become the center, we have seen many

homes in many parts of the country show forth His power. If one invites the Living Christ to enter, wonderful changes take place, and His peace and power exert a strong influence. Even unsuspecting souls often say they "feel something" in such a house. Of course, Christ is everywhere, but when we consciously ask His Presence and leading, we experience a deeper awareness of Him.

Fortunately, in our new home we had built several extra bedrooms and were, therefore, able to have frequent guests in this period. Some lived with us for months at a time, and we had rich experiences in spiritual fellowship as well as in examples of spiritual rebirth and healing. We were indeed blessed to be a small part of this group work and to have our home used in this way. We made numerous mistakes and had much to learn, but these years in our lives were especially rewarding ones because, no matter how imperfectly, we were attempting to become channels for His love to others.

16

THE FINISHED PICTURE

On Mother's Day, 1942, I was convalescing from a major operation. Furthermore, my brother was in a Washington hospital very sick after serious surgery, and I was receiving alarming letters about his condition. Once again this was a period of illness and personal testing. Once again, we see how our loved ones on the other side come to our aid in our times of trouble and sickness.

Coronado, California
May 10, 1942

"Dear Mom, this is Mother's Day and I remember my wonderful mother; however, today is not different from any other except that love is intensified by the power of suggestion. This day brings so much thought of mother, the greatest earth symbol of love, that power is increased. As at Christmas and Easter when love of our Master is more concentrated, the highest vibrations are set in motion and new power is released. Thus it is that any emotion whatsoever becomes intensified. Therefore, you must never give power to destructive thinking because it adds to the momentum of evil.

"Right now you are going through a test, but you will pass with a big margin. We are all pulling for you, and our love is hovering about you like a mantle of protection. You will soon be able to play tennis again and to chase around Los Angeles looking for hats, Mom. You are absorbing

*health physically, mentally and spiritually. I did not come
into your consciousness when you were very ill because I
am too close to your emotions.*

*"Tell Aunt May that we on this side are helping her and
that the tide for Uncle Roy will soon turn. Do not ever
think or express negative thoughts about him. The correct
visualization, trust and love from all of you are helping to
lift him. He is in danger, but only from the mental mists
of despondency around him. You must all strive to counter-
act these poisons. We are helping to guide his doctors by
injecting suggestions into their minds. You must assist us
by bathing him in light, love and peace.*

*"Mom, you are a mere child, you must wake up and
utilize the power which is available to you. Life has not
hurt the real you, it can never do that. It has merely given
you a better grasp of realities. None of you dear ones can
slip back for long for, when any of you feel downward pulls,
we here are a strong unit reacting instantaneously to help
you back on the right path.*

*"Do not let earthly shadows of war, or anything else,
shake your faith. We are all living in the Creator's finished
picture. All is planned, prepared and perfected. We can
see this by peeling off ages of doubt, hate and selfishness.
Many on earth are now seeing real values; scales of illusion
and blindness are falling from the world's eyes as the vision
unfolds. Help it to unfold more quickly by seeing only
beauty (God's vision), truth (His voice) and light (His
love).*

*"Rest and get well, Mom. You know I love you. Happy
Day."*

17

GOD NEEDS HUMAN CHANNELS

More than two busy wartime years have passed since the last message from Lowell. In my mind several facts from this era stand out. They lead, directly or indirectly, to my growing interest in spiritual healing. Franklin had developed a heart condition which was the cause of his often-repeated stays in the hospital. My own physical limitations also brought distress and, in addition, led me to many questions and to many exciting conclusions. In my Gray Lady work more questions arose. I became convinced that even the best care and medical attention available are still not enough, that love is essential for complete healing. My heart ached when cases were called hopeless; surely our Master never knew the meaning of such a word. Surely faith could "make men whole" in this age as in earlier ages—faith, prayer and belief in a God to Whom "all things are possible," a God of Love in whom wholeness and health are synonomous.

At this point in my personal spiritual life, my future thinking and growth began to be strongly influenced by Ethel and John Gayner Banks, those valiant workers in the field of spiritual healing. Their dedication was contagious, as was their faith in the absolute power and in the un-qualified eagerness of our Lord to "heal the sick." They believed, too, that His Will, as His life demonstrates, is never anything less than wholeness of body, mind and spirit. They refused to limit His power and stressed that healing was an integral part of Christ's mission on earth and of His command to us to preach the gospel and heal the sick. I am increasingly aware of the importance of their belief that divine healing rightfully belongs as an accepted and respected part of the church.

Being acutely aware of Franklin's and my physical problems, having constantly before me the needs of our servicemen in the hospital where I worked, knowing many losses and war tragedies in our predominately Navy town—all these provided impetus to my awakening interest in Christian healing. My compassion was aroused by the seemingly endless chain of suffering in our strife-torn world. To spread the "good news" of the healing love of the Risen Christ, as all-powerful today as when He lived on earth, became an insistent desire.

Prayer was now growing to be more important in every area of my life, and the realization was born in me that even I could become a channel for Christ's healing power. I was a member of the intercessory prayer group in our church. In my Gray Lady work I often used prayer quietly and with deepening faith in its results. In other words, spiritual healing had not only aroused my enthusiasm and intellectual acceptance but was becoming significantly emphasized in my daily and personal life.

Coronado, California
July 14, 1944

"Do not ever be afraid or anxious, Mom, your pathway leads toward the light. The climb has been a bit hard on your emotions and health, but you are now reaching a new level. The future is bright for both of you; your most useful years are coming. Many frustrations have taught you more of tolerance, patience and love. These will stay with you

even when the difficult situations and circumstances are forgotten.

"You need to be quiet more often and to listen more inside. It is harmful and unintelligent to get so tired that you cannot hear the inner voice, which is God speaking. Breathe more deeply and throw away fear by losing yourself in trust and service. Dad is doing too much mental work. He must relax and laugh more.

"Junie is fine, but he must not permit discouraging thoughts to enter his mind. He must look out more instead of within so much. I will do all I can to help influence him, but he needs earth-love and understanding, too. Please write him and tell him to stand firm, holding his dreams in a tightly closed box until the time comes to release and enjoy them.

"We must all serve. Oh, how rejoiceful we will be when evil lags with weariness! Evil cannot win. It has unseen wounds now and knows it is losing, that is why it is so desperate. God's chosen children can patiently await His time because they have the inner peace and assurance to carry them through any hell.

"What an experience life is—what a joy, no matter where it is! In an earth soul, in a spirit, in a flying bird or in a tiny flower, it is always life—life eternal. Be grateful for it every minute of everyday and give life to all you touch. That is the secret of happiness. I bless the awareness of life which is growing in you and Dad. I bless its coming in greater degree as you give it forth. It is indeed true that Christ brings more abundant life and health. Consecrated lives must always be channels for the love and healing of the Master. He alone provides the flow and the current. He alone 'doeth the works.' You two must ever be ready to pass on the love and joy which come to you from the

invisible world. Thus does light come into man-made dark-ness. As the light flows freely, joy and peace which pass man's understanding permeate the awakening world."

18

FOGS OF DOUBT

One fact becomes clearer to me as I think about the next writing. It is how much closer to the church we now had grown. Strangely, my father's strong spiritual beliefs had not communicated themselves to me while he was alive. Despite regular church attendance and choir membership in my youth, my personal religion had remained shadowy. Although my father had been an army chaplain and a minister who lived the love he preached, not until this period in my life, long after his death, did I begin to appreciate his wonderful faith and Christian strength. Often in those days my father's influence was belatedly touching my heart and life, as his memory came into clearer focus and was better understood. Both Franklin and I had been brought up in the church, and Lowell had always gone to Sunday School and been active in its affairs. As I have mentioned before, Lowell also sang in the choir, but Franklin and I did not attend services regularly in those earlier years of our marriage. We had not known the value of worshipping with others. Now at last we began to understand that the church is actually the Body of Christ and hence the channel to bring about God's plan for mankind. Our own church had gradually come to assume a vital place in our lives. From feverish days of war, from worldly duties and gatherings, we increasingly turned to it, to its strength and comfort, to its fellowship. We became more active in its work, and now Franklin was serving as senior warden.

Not surprising is the fact that I usually felt very close to Lowell in church, and often his messages came to me there.

Coronado, California
September, 1944

"Mom, I am doing something new. I am trying to be a lifter of the pressure in the world. I want to help lift the ugly darkness hiding you from us. Clouds of vapor are shutting off, or dimming, our vision of earth. Great scientists here are working to induce earth power to co-operate with us. Their purpose is to create a great-enough and powerful-enough light to pierce the darkness. The light must be in yourselves; the darkness is caused by doubt and fear, and we must try together to dispel it.

"The gases and fumes from earth are deadly and have to be cleared away. You must believe that we are trying to help, and you must co-operate more. Our thoughts can travel to your minds, but then even you, Mom, sometimes doubt their origin. Oh, Mom, do you not know that it is I speaking in your mind? I am still Lowell, only I cannot go back to your way of explaining things. My way is to inject thought-power into you, but the fogs are all around you today. Only once in a while can I see you plainly. It must be either that you are doubting or that you are not alert enough.

"Quietness and prayer help to clear the way. That is why I can come closer to you in church. To dispel the fogs you must know in your heart that life has no end. You all are so cramped by your bodies that I sometimes feel sorry for you. Can you understand that? I am insoluble energy now. I am also able to pierce certain minds on your plane and to lift them to my plane of thought. I am trying to help Uncle Percival (scientist in Washington doing research

work). We need minds like his to work through. All scientists are especially needed today in order that we may teach the right use of the power that is to come."

19

INCREASING AWARENESS

After years of communications from my spirit son and
a growing awareness of the spiritual side of life, I was becoming more conscious all the time of two worlds. Keeping
up with both our old world and our newer world of spirit
was now growing more difficult. Therefore, a pulling from
one to the other often occurred, but gradually we were relinquishing many former interests. To some, our abandon-
ment of worthwhile worldly interests may have seemed "ill-
advised" as Lowell suggests, but we were learning the importance of distinguishing the best or highest from the
merely good. This, I believe, explains Lowell's reference to
our "new work" in the following message.

The Mrs. Morse* mentioned had a son who was Lowell's
contemporary. The boy had just been killed in a tragic
accident, and I felt I should show her some of Lowell's
messages. By now I dared not go against such definite
urging as I felt in this matter. I remember how reluctant I
was that day to read my intimate writings to Mrs. Morse,
but I am glad I made myself do so. I may never know
how much my obedience and Lowell's words helped her,
but often in this life we are not privileged to see the con-
sequences of our own guidance and its ensuing actions. If
we always understood causes and results how could our
faith develop strength and steadfastness? "Faith is the substance of things hoped for, the evidence of things not seen."

---

* See Preface.

Coronado, California
January 18, 1945

*"Mom, do not be surprised at any new developments.
Earth's pains are acute, but here we see healing coming on
the wings of tears and suffering. The new dawn is already
streaking a blackened sky with the faint aurora of the
promised enlightened day.*

*"Yes, you and Dad are coming into a new work; all be-
fore has been training. To worldly eyes, it may seem ill-
advised, but in the eyes of God's chosen it is a new adventure in faith and a new level of service. Have no fear, even
though you both sense change. Have no feeling of being
tied to material things or even to your home which is being
used by souls who are spreading the light. Much potential
power is right at your doorstep, and you are becoming more
aware of it.*

*"No, Mom, you don't talk too much. You never know
why you say and do impulsive things, but I know. Many
times we are working through you, and it is all part of a
plan beyond your power to comprehend. Don't worry about
Mrs. Morse, I influenced you to see her. I know her boy,
and he was dazed at first and unhappy at his mother's grief.
He wants her to know he is still alive. He loved life and
dreamed great dreams, but now he is beginning to see that
real dreams will come true sooner here than on earth.*

*"Mrs. Morse is unconsciously fighting her intuitive be-
liefs, but she has great possibilities of service. Her path
leads to a mountain peak. Although her climb now is slow
and discouraging, suddenly she will reach the top and will
be dazzled by its glory. She will see both sides as a revelation and will understand that her long climb was necessary
to see the entire view of eternal beauty.*

"Mom, don't rush around so much. Be still and send out

your prayer desires. You can be of more use that way. You must rest and be sensitive to all of us who are working with you. We need you even more than you need us. Your experience last night with Mrs. Morse was just one more tug from the invisibles to align your efforts in the right direction.

"Life is never lost, nor hurt, nor thwarted. It goes on forever, attracting more life like a magnet. It is only the human mind which separates men from their best selves. Life is everywhere, pulsating within and without. We are daily injecting it into you and Dad. Think of our influence as a spiritual transfusion which stimulates the bodily functions, sharpens the mind and, above all, sensitizes the spirit-ego to know its own true course.

"I am everywhere; I come and go as thought, for there is no time, nor space, nor limitation in the spirit's wanderings. You know I am with you and Dad, and the time is coming soon when we must work more consciously together.

"Bless you! I am leading you always on the Christ Ray, the cosmic light ray of the earth. Rejoice, be gay and happy; do not be depressed because the earth is dark and filled with war, discord and suffering. Rather, be lifted up because you know the earth will emerge from this static state into a dawn of newer consciousness."

20

MOTHER SPEAKS ACROSS

On the very same day in January, 1945, I wrote the following message from my mother. In the same way that Lowell's messages begin with "Mom, Mom, Mom," my mother's start with the ringing words, "Praise God from whom all blessings flow." Although she herself did not possess the gift of intuitive writing, my mother believed wholeheartedly in my writing. She had always encouraged me and urged me to develop and use that ability. She and Lowell had personalities somewhat alike. They were full of enthusiasm for life, and they shared a great love of adventure. Now from the other side they were both working to help us and were pressing us on to higher development. On this day, the same emphasis and truth, but expressed very differently, came to me from my son and his grandmother.

Mother left this life after 90 full and active years. A minister's wife, the mother of four children, she was always an individualist and never conformed to matter-of-fact living. She kept her enthusiasm and love of life until the end. Ever interested in learning something new, she had pronounced ideas and many fascinating facets of mind and personality. Never one to accept limitations, she lived life to the utmost even at an advanced age. Until she went out of this life, she was alert and keenly interested in the lives of others and in the affairs of the larger world. Finally the time came for our wonderfully vital mother to leave us. Her life flickered out one night as she slept, but her brave and adventurous spirit goes on to greater glories and to greater service.

Coronado, California
January 18, 1945

"Praise God from whom all blessings flow:

"My daughter, I am happy that now we can use the gift you have had since childhood, your spiritual sensitivity to Eternal urgings. Yes, you were often a will-of-the-wisp, but now you are nearer your true course which is lighted by the reflection of the great lamp on the altar of time-lessness. Your own light is faint, but as we work together to usher in the era of the coming Christ, you will reflect more power and a steadier light. When one is alight, the lost will come like moths to a flame. When one is truly alive, the sick, discouraged and broken will draw near that life. When one is deeply silent, soul voices will speak in that silence. Be thankful and full of adoration for your contact with the invisible world, and a great symphony of God's choir will sing through you.

"I am with you, my children. Love each other and respect each other's way of development. We will all meet because all paths of truth converge, even though we do not know where. We know that all children of God will one day be merged even as scattered quicksilver merges into a ball of limpid beauty."

21

CHRIST-POWER WITHIN

To the emphasis of the next message on Christ and the
power within, I would add only that Lowell is trying to tell
us how to find and use more effectively that power available for help in the tragic and demanding times in which
we were living. We had long used prayer and tried to be
channels of love in a suffering world; yet, we often became
exhausted and aware of inadequacy when faced with the
urgent needs all around us. More complete dependence on
God, on the Christ within, was the only answer, as we read
in this message.

As I worked as a volunteer in a Navy hospital, the seemingly endless number of casualties and the terrible suffering
I witnessed naturally impressed me profoundly. The ampu-
tations, the paralyzed bodies, the mentally injured, the
shell-shocked begin the list, but the utter despair I often
saw was beyond description. I spent much time in the
plastic surgery ward, and there war seemed to have fulfilled
its evil worst. One of the finest plastic surgeons in the country was in charge, a wonderful man, and we quietly and
secretly tried to keep him and his work undergirded with
prayer. Prayer was used in all my work in the hospital but,
of course, never openly. I knew that God's love was essential for any complete healing and that prayer was a vital
factor in the healing of attitudes, human relationships and
broken spirits as well as of wounded bodies. Surely the
source of courage and all renewal lies in God, and no prob-

lem in any area is ever too large or too small to bring to His Love. Eventually, we saw some amazing things occur, and unexpected avenues of help and healing opened many times. I shall never forget, for example, the paralyzed boy whose case had been considered medically hopeless and whose despair had been almost total. Yet one day a faint bit of life came into his toes. His condition went on to improve and, finally, he was sent to another hospital for more advanced treatment and care. Although I lost track of his case, faith told me that his healing continued.

Coronado also knew many bereaved homes in these war years, and over and over prayer seemed the one possible way in which help could be given. Despite our experience in prayer with its tangible and intangible, its seen and its unseen answers, our faith often slipped as we relied too much on our own strength and not completely enough on God. Faced with tragedy and anguish in so many places and often faced with lack of faith and with reliance on worldly means alone, one can imagine both my need for and the beneficial results of words like the following from Lowell.

Coronado, California
June, 1945

"Mom, inharmony is the devil's keen weapon. Inharmony throws reason off balance. Be not a part of imbalance, for you have work to do. Do not allow any human's point of view to swerve you from your sense of direction. You have all you need within your own secret chamber to teach you and guide you. Rely only on the Christ-within-you. Listen to others' words, but always check them with the inner voice. You are blessed with an inner direction-finder which will steer you through fogs of doubt and through

stormy seas of men's chatterings. Be true to its urgings and ignore the world's noisiness. Many would-be seekers are intercepted by confusing forces because they are not securely anchored in Christ-consciousness. Seek only His staying power of peace. There is no force in the Cosmic World as strong as divine love.

"Christ's love integrates personalities and brings wholeness to body, mind and spirit. It brightens every twist and turn on Life's road. It recharges worn cells of body and mind, it compensates for all limitations. Through it, all negatives are resurrected into positives. It is the hidden power of all life.

"Many souls are not attuned to receive this love-power directly. They must receive it through a human channel until they themselves seek and learn the laws of attunement to love. Do not ponder too much over this. Accept with joy your own capacity to receive vibrations of love; relay them to others as you are inwardly directed, even when it is not as your human will might choose.

"Light is the absence of shadow-darkness. Be so filled with Light and Love that shadows of earth personalities will be dissolved. I will be in your thoughts in sleep tonight to bless them and to cleanse them with cosmic radiations. Sweet dreams, Mom."

22

EMPATHY

In April, 1946, my husband was retired from active duty for physical disability. With retirement his health improved steadily and surely. With more time to devote to spiritual life, with increasing physical energy and fewer material or financial problems, our life pattern began to follow a new rhythm.

We were planning to return to Maine for the summer for the first time since Lowell's death, a period of ten years. We love Maine, its crispness, its healing freshness and its unique combination of independence and friendliness, of sturdiness and beauty. Maine is part of us and is forever calling us back to the gentle coves and the sweeping tides of our favorite section of Casco Bay. A huge purple lilac bush above our cottage always welcomes us to a world of newness and ecstatic growing, and when we reluctantly leave, our wistful hearts are warmed by the glory of autumn's coloring.

I realize now that Lowell was drawing us back to our beloved Maine. He knew better than we how beneficial it would be for us and also that future happiness and service were in store for us there. Despite many misgivings, we felt a great longing to go, but in contrast to the inner urging to make the trip, we received much human advice against it. Of course we ourselves were somewhat concerned about the possible bad effects of old memories and associations. Yet, through prayer we were able to conquer our doubts and now were beginning to make definite plans for the trip to Maine.

Coronado, California
January, 1946

"Dear Mom, you and Dad are to have greater freedom from material and physical limitations, and you will then be better prepared to help us here. We have been eagerly awaiting this time. I am glad you are going back to Maine. You are being led, and it is much easier to lead you now.

"The time for closer contact with earth forces is drawing nearer. A new ray will be discovered in which one human vibration can be tapped into another, thus may thoughts and even conversations be exchanged. We have worked hard here and are now contacting souls to be used when the new ray is launched. Only those serving their highest spiritual urges will be sensitive enough. It will be on a higher spiritual level than clairvoyance or thought transference.

"You and Dad can help in this new field. We will have fun and you will be overjoyed by this new development. The whole earth is holding its breath and does not know why tension is so prevalent. It is being tested and timed in the new force. Relax and enjoy every minute of this time, for much work is ahead—joyful, potent work. I am with you always."

Of course I have no way of knowing as a certainty, but I strongly suspect that Lowell's mention here of a "new ray" refers to the power of a highly developed empathy. This power seems to grow in conjunction with spiritual development. Thinking of others with love definitely increases our capacity to understand them. We all know, for example, that nothing draws people closer together than prayer and spiritual bonds. My dictionary gives as one definition for empathy, "Appreciative perception and understanding," and I can add from my own life that empathy can be an astounding experience in the spiritual realm. Often one senses another's needs and emotions to a remarkable extent. Christ alone sees deeply enough into men's souls to make a perfect diagnosis. As instruments in Christ's service, we, faulty and weak as we are, are given some of His perception and understanding. The more selfless our love, it seems, the keener become our faculties with which to comprehend the inner needs of our fellow men and thus better to serve them and our Master.

23

LIVING PERSONALITIES

God is life. God is energy. That was a hard lesson for me
to absorb and is one I am still working on. In the next message, Lowell mentions my "unbounded enthusiasm" which
often causes me to squander the priceless gift of God's
energy. I can see clearly now that I have retarded my spiritual growth as well as complete physical healing because I
have not sufficiently recognized the body as the "temple of
the spirit." Discipline and good stewardship have been lacking. Too often I have listened to the demands and needs of
men rather than to God within. To me, doing good things
seemed to imply that there would always be plenty of
energy for those purposes. I have not been selective enough
nor learned to do only those things which are mine to do.
There are countless good causes as there are countless souls
in need of love. Not one of us can answer all calls or give
of ourselves to anything but the minutest fraction of the
whole. Because a work is good or worthwhile is not an infallible reason for expending energy on it. In the guided
life, not only must we choose to live up to the best and
highest we know, but we must become very sensitive to
which tasks are meant for us.

As man himself is threefold, so is his energy of body,
mind and spirit. When life, or energy, is lacking in one, all
three suffer. In the same way, when one area is over-
emphasized and the others neglected, the results are unhappy and painful. Balance is a law of life, and God gives

us wisdom and guidance so that we can seek with confidence its perfection and wholeness.

Lowell is apparently telling me in the next message that truth is truth, regardless of the channel used. For a long time now I had been wondering why Lowell's messages were often impersonal and sometimes did not even sound like him. The answer appeared to have two aspects. First, other souls were occasionally speaking to me through him; secondly, my son's spirit was becoming more universal in scope and in service.

Coronado, California
April 18, 1946

"You sense my nearness tonight, Mom, because I am hovering around you. I love to go along with you and Dad in your thoughts. Actually I am fused in your thoughts, and I come in such instantaneous response that you feel as if I were talking to you. I do talk in your heart often—such bright, happy hearts you and Dad have! They are like mine except that mine holds larger vistas. I see the effect of things even before you see the cause.

"You must go more slowly, Mom, to conserve your reserve energy. You can always replenish your spirit energy, for spirit is endless, tireless and limitless, but your body must obey nature's laws if you are to keep it a fit place for that unbounded enthusiasm of yours.

"There are entities here who are attuned to you and who will teach you new truths. Sometimes I shall be the beacon ray to transmit these lessons; sometimes you will receive them directly from higher souls. You are fortunate to be chosen, but you can be used more effectively if you are physically strong and mentally quiet.

"Please go to see Mrs. Andrews*. She is a sensitive soul and could be a channel to help others. She needs rest, for her thoughts are perpetually in turmoil. She should talk from her heart, not from her suppressed mind. Help her to release unhappy memories, her son has no unhappy memories. His going was swift and without pain. He wants his mother to know that he did not suffer and that he is well and happy the way she saw him in her dream. Sometimes dreams are more real than waking thoughts, for released minds can flow into reality or into eternity, whereas controlled-by-self, wakeful minds are stifled by everyday living. She has great happiness ahead, for her son is her guide; she is receiving increasing wisdom through him. Please believe in us and talk to us because we are living personalities. We live, move and think just as we always have, but now in a world invisible to your eyes. We are real only to those who love us and who keep warm inner fires burning.

"Enlightened minds are going to be used as never before. Book learning is not always necessary, but inner receptivity is priceless. Develop this quality and the results will astonish you. I am going to figure out a way to reach you more clearly in your dreams, so ask for an open mind to catch penetrating thoughts from me tonight."

Following Lowell's request, I went to see Mrs. Andrews, whom I found to be in a very depressed state of mind. Her son, an aviator during the war, was first reported missing in action and then later declared dead. One night he appeared to her and knelt beside her bed, saying he was still alive and happy and asking his mother not to grieve for him any longer. Not believing such a contact possible, the mother was afraid she was losing her sanity and, until my

---

* See Preface.

visit, had not dared to tell anyone of her experience. Being led to talk to her about Lowell and our communication, I was thus used to open the door of understanding and release for her.

Lowell emphasizes that the continuity of life in the face of physical death is a natural condition of creation, in fact, is reality itself. However, man has often made the continuity and especially the contact between the two worlds to appear unnatural, morbid or eerie. Abuse and exploitation of the power and means of communication have contributed to this unhealthy condition. Mercenary motives and deceit have also done great harm. In addition, self-pity and self-centered thinking bring disruption here, as elsewhere, and threaten to injure the invisible bond between worlds. Natural and wholesome as is believing in and knowing the nearness and presence of loved ones from the next world, we obviously should not try to pull them back for mere personal solace or for any selfish reason.

We all receive intuitive impulses and thoughts, but some souls are more sensitive to them than others, just as some are better aware of their source. Christ is the Source as He is the Center, but clearly He works in and through souls at all stages of development in the continuity of life. As we grow closer to the Source, we naturally grow more conscious of and more obedient to any leadings He gives us through any of the countless means at His disposal.

As Lowell warns against ignoring or discounting the inner voice, I would go a step further and plead for better understanding of our invisible helpers. After learning the nature of this book, many friends have secretly told me of their own experiences of contact with loved ones who have passed on. The number of such confidants has been amazing. Each has helped to strengthen my own faith, and we all gain release and confidence through sharing with sympathetic listeners our experiences and the truth that there is no death, that not even loss of communication or contact need exist. We are all living in God's "eternal now;" yet, unhappily, so many still have ears and do not hear, eyes and do not see.

24

ETERNAL ECHOES

During the anthem on Easter Sunday that year, I wrote the following message from Lowell on the church calendar. It was a glorious day, and I was very conscious of Easter gladness. I was also aware of Lowell's nearness and of the resultant heightening of my joy. A beautiful and appropriate anthem of rejoicing was being sung, and Lowell's voice seemed to be mingling with those of the singers. I could feel his joy, his celestial laughter and love uniting with the exultation of the choir and the congregation.

That morning's experience and Lowell's words made me realize as never before the great power that is generated by masses coming together "in one accord" to praise and glorify God. In my heart and mind another fact was stressed. When we have released our loved ones of the next world to their new life and work, when we do not hold them back by excessive pondering and selfish grief, then can we catch the rhythm of their contagious joy. On such days as Easter, the two worlds meet in holy praise and worship. Our rapture mingles with theirs, and the echoes are eternal. We are all lifted up together with Christ. "And I, if I be lifted up, shall draw all men to me."

Christ Church
Coronado, California
April 20, 1946

"Dearest Mom:
    "What a happy day! Peace, joy and life are being poured

into earth souls. More than ever before in creation are we uniting, one plane with another. The great Life Force is increasingly fluid and is coming from the all-power center to God's chosen servants. From souls on higher planes this force passes through us and on to you on earth. All men shall be lifted up. Oh! Mom, I am being lifted up. I see clearer pathways ahead of me, and the shadowy pathways on earth are growing brighter, too, as new lights appear to guide men.

"Can't you hear me singing today? I am in the Easter anthems. I am in harmony with such beautiful music that I tingle with joy. Sing, all you on earth, so that your songs of inner joy shall mingle with ours until evil is disintegrated. Evil cannot stand against love and joy. Music, like harmonious thoughts, creates positive vibrations which are destructive to evil.

"Evil is far from defeated but, on days like today, when in all the countries of the world men raise their minds and hearts toward God, a greater light force rises from the earth and is attracted to our cosmic radiations. Someday these forces will actually merge; we must all work consciously for that day. Every soul who yearns for God is helping to increase the rate of uplift.

"You must love life, both its action and its rest; each is necessary for balance, which is the regulator of power. Gray days in contrast to sparkling days, like today, teach this balance.

"Be lifted up. I am your happiness and your protecting inner balance. I am a channel through which God pours out His blessing and love. Be happy and have no fears so that you can reflect greater peace and joy. My love sings into your hearts. We are together now and always."

25

WE RETURN TO MAINE

When the next message was written, we were finally, after surmounting many difficulties, on the way to Maine. Throughout the long, cross-country, motor trip, we were often conscious of God's nearness. We also felt convinced that the trip and the return to Maine were right and what we were meant to do. From all points of view, it was right for Franklin to have a change and a vacation, for he had not had any leave, except sick-leave, in the last seven years.

It is interesting to note here that Lowell checks us a bit and gives us cause to think about our attitude toward the coming months. We were looking forward to our stay in Maine as a time to loaf, to enjoy ourselves and to forget responsibility. Lowell is warning us of the peril of "love for humanity" deteriorating into "self-centered love." The two of us were apparently in danger of living too much unto ourselves. In our contentment and satisfaction with our personal spiritual life, were we as outgoing and as outgiving as we should be? Was anticipation of our summer in Maine leading us into the mistake of a more worldly than spiritual approach? This was perhaps a natural error, but before our own spirits saw, our spirit-son recognized the trap into which we were falling.

Washington, D. C.
May 30, 1946

"Mom, I told you we would make it together. A lovely

mantle of light surrounds you like an impregnable garment. Nothing can harm the real you if your heart and mind are at peace and in accord with positive, vital, love-infused currents.

"Your pathway is clear. Focus on that, not on material upsets. Follow the pathway of cosmic, recreative light rays. The sun is always shining even though you cannot see it. As it shines eternally, so does the love principle ever pour from infinite center into spirit center.

"Praise God day and night for the eternal glow, and ask that more and more of it shall flow into your minds and bodies. It is healing, it is inspiration, it is loving understanding. It is constructive to the good of all mankind. Your different life in Maine this summer will try to shake your love for humanity into self-centered love. We must live for all, not for ourselves alone; that is the secret of peace. God sees the heart's desire; therefore, His power comes to the attuned, whether or not they are conscious of it. We need all power, all minds and all prayers to win.

"We three need each other; we love each other, but we need to love Light more. May God's blessings fall endlessly and increasingly into you both. I am here and there and everywhere, for I, too, follow the great Light and live to inject it more deeply into earth minds and hearts. Nothing is impossible if you are a positive conductor of eternal Light and Love. Shine and sing, Mom."

A few weeks after this message we arrived in Maine. Strangely, after having felt right all the time about our trip, within ten miles of our destination a sudden mood of depression came over us both. Old memories, fear that we had made a mistake in coming, and dread of the summer itself attacked us. Accordingly, we stopped the car to have a prayer of renewal, a prayer for strength and courage.

We had parked at the side of a little bridge which affords a particularly lovely view of a quiet stream with a few weathered homes and Maine's ever-present pines peacefully reproduced in its water.

"He leadeth me beside the still waters." Our panicky dejection lasted but a few moments, for almost instantly reassurance came that all was well. During our minutes of quiet, I was vividly affected by Lowell's spirit. I could hear his happy voice ringing in my mind and saying, "Everything will be all right, Mom. You will be glad you came."

Thereafter we drove a few miles in silence. Feeling deeply moved and uplifted, I did not at first notice that Franklin had also been stirred by strong emotion. When I regained enough composure to tell him the happy story of Lowell's words, I was astounded to have him reveal an even more thrilling experience which had taken place simultaneously with mine. To Franklin his son appeared to be standing beside the car. Smiling radiantly, Lowell spoke to his father in words similar to those he had given me. "Everything is O.K., Dad, and you will love Maine again." Immediately, confidence and joy swept over my husband.

Our release from troubled thoughts and our happiness were more profound because of the joyful realization that Lowell had come to us both this time. Now no shadows of doubt remained in our hearts about our return to Maine.

This year we had rented a Sebasco cottage in which we had never lived before, yet it became home to us almost at once. I suppose we should not have been surprised, but we certainly were delighted upon opening the door for the first time to discover a large and beautiful bouquet of purple lilacs to greet us. Once again our hearts were full; in previous Junes, Lowell had enjoyed gathering fragrant blossoms for us from the same huge lilac bush on the hill. This year other hands had cut the flowers, but nothing could possibly have made us feel more at home than the sight and scent of those lilacs. I gasped with excitement when I discovered on the same table with the flowers a little Mexican ash tray which was almost an exact duplicate of one Lowell had given me his last Christmas on earth.

The final welcoming or homecoming touch was to turn on the radio and to hear the familiar strains of one of Lowell's favorite songs. A bit incredulously, yet with happy acceptance of unseen reality, we smiled into each other's eyes. We delightedly acknowledged Lowell's presence with us, as we instinctively and readily recognized his contagious, mischievous joy all about us.

26

MAN MUST CHOOSE

Now that Franklin had retired, he was becoming increasingly engrossed in his hobby of writing, and my interest in the same subject was also being stimulated. Not until eight years later did we begin to follow Lowell's suggestions of the next message and to work together on this present book. Once again Lowell saw long before we the shadow of coming events, and fortunately the patience of the next world is endless! Although we did not realize the eventual course of our work, we spent hours writing and re-writing poetry, short stories and articles. In addition, many intuitive messages came to me on healing and on world affairs; during these months in Maine words of personal training also filled literally dozens of pages.

Sebasco Estates, Maine
July 10, 1946

"Mom and Dad, at last you begin to understand. Together you two can work with me much more effectively. I have been trying to ask Dad for a long time to help with our writings. His mind and his larger vocabulary are needed for some of the ideas we wish to convey to you. Naturally, the more minds in harmony we have, the better are we able to express ourselves.

"Universal mind currents are healing, constructive and vital in the great work of merging the two planes. We know that no mind ever dies. We are eager to learn from higher

entities here, but many on earth still seem to think of words from our plane as some form of mysterious, perhaps un-balanced, thinking. True balance never asserts itself in the individual unless his mental, physical and spiritual faculties are co-ordinated and co-operative. It is the same in your world where no community nor government can function effectively unless there is harmony in individual minds. Neither will the world family ever live in peace and pros-perity until each nation is awakened to the fact that it is a part of the whole. Furthermore, the continued existence of mankind will not evolve as God intends until your world is educated to believe in the necessity of closer co-operation between all planes of existence, especially between our plane and your earth plane. We must pull together. Then the higher souls who know reality will be free to express through us more of the truth of life.

"All life is a struggle and a school where Truth, which is God, is assimilated. As a child cannot understand before he studies and acquires knowledge, so spiritual man cannot be led to an understanding of eternal values until he listens to and obeys the higher urges.

"Intuitive wisdom does not come from books or from finite minds, but from thought-currents of souls who are using their present existence to fulfill the laws of the uni-verse. Truth, once learned, must be re-expressed to make its currents flow rhythmically. If one clutches truth and does not express it, one is serving self rather than the whole; thus is progress blocked.

"Men who think impulses start within the human mind are mistaken. There is only one consciousness, and science is daily proving that oneness. When one thinks only of self, one loses this current-contact and thus is lost temporarily to the great plan of the Creator. This separation is commonly

called evil; however, evil is in reality the wrong use of free will. Each man chooses, but many do not choose to revert to the original plan which embraces all. Whatever hurts one, hurts all; whatever enlightens one, enlightens all. We are indissolubly linked with the laws of creative mind, whose essence is love and harmony.

"Earth souls must be taught the power of an harmonious, loving-all thought, and that the real lesson of life is to learn to be outflowing and receptive to life currents rather than to death currents. Life or stagnation, good or evil, love or hate, between these free man must choose. Few men use their minds to choose aright. They have allowed their minds, which are their receiving and relaying stations, to become clogged and thus unfit to absorb the vital currents of truth. Since time began, misdirected use of free will has caused the evils of the universe.

"All great prophets have brought the same message in one way or another. Christ, the Son of God, has given us a textbook of the laws of the universe in His Sermon On The Mount. Yet, man, smug in his belief that he thinks, invents and discovers through his own power, has retarded for thousands of years the purposes of time. Spiritual laws are not mere religion; they are the secret powers of the universe. Revelations are waiting to be released if and when men link up with All-Mind.

"You must use this power, Mom, don't wait for demonstrations. I will work with you whenever you ask. I have a larger capacity than you for indrawing of creative Mind because I have no physical handicaps. Less and less will your bodies retard you as spiritual laws are absorbed."

27

LAUGHTER IN THE MIND

The night before the next message, Lowell's vivid laughter had come to me in a dream. Of course I often saw him in dreams, but this was different. For the first time, I seemed actually to hear his voice; his happy laughter was clear to me just as if he were still my earthly child who had come to my room to awaken me with his gay, laughing voice. The results of this impressive experience carried over into the morning, for I was still tingling with joy such as must be Lowell's. I think I felt as if I had been more truly with my son in spirit than ever before in the ten years since he had gone on to the next world. The realistic echoes of his happiness made me more conscious of the endless dimensions of joyous freedom in which Lowell's spirit now dwells.

The exhilaration and deep satisfaction which came to me from hearing Lowell's laughter and from sensing its vital meaning were, I am sure, connected with my unexpected viewing of the Bath Hospital. Better than I can, Lowell explains in the following message how he had influenced me to go there a few days earlier so that a still-painful memory could be erased.

Although I had so far avoided conscious thought or any sight of the hospital, it is true that a deep-seated aversion and near-fear of that building and its associations remained in me. For ten days I had helplessly watched my child suffer and die there, and I would not have chosen deliberately to bring back the memory of those agonizing days.

However, Lowell, wiser than I, recognized the need of ridding my subconscious of buried pain and grief.

One day I strangely lost my way while driving in the small and familiar city of Bath. Suddenly I found myself in front of the hospital, only to discover that my fears were unfounded. The power of the ten-year-old memories no longer existed. Even here where I had known such agony, I could now experience joy! I also felt a very real gratitude for having discovered this fact and for having been led to the one place I still dreaded, thus clearing the last hurdle of unhappiness in connection with Lowell's passing.

Sebasco Estates, Maine
August 3, 1946

"Mom, you heard me laugh last night, and I am glad. What you heard was indeed real and is a sign of progress for you. Of course I am laughing; I am tingling with joy because you are nearer me and my happiness.

"You conquered the last vestige of your physical longing for me when you drove by the Bath Hospital. I knew that was the last tie in your subconscious mind which was binding you to the grief of my passing. No chance made you take the wrong road that day. I influenced you to go that way so that you would know, once and for all, that you can face any difficult earth task and, facing it, be freed from its pain and sorrow. My bodily pain and suffering are no longer real for the simple reason that they do not exist. It is only I—living, loving, laughing, closer than the walls about you—that is real. Death is not the end nor numbness of life but is release, joy and realness.

"As you live more in this glad consciousness, you shall be a better means of relaying truth to those who live only in the material world. They are the dreamers, the mute, the

inarticulate, whereas those who live with us in reality are the triumphant, the wise, the released ones. There is a great need on this side for awakened-to-reality souls. Years of worldly thinking, of doubting and of demanding logical explanations and proof have built such a wall between the two worlds that we cannot reach across to help as we wish.

"Only to the awakened, who are linked with divine purpose and eternal mind, who are burning with desire to reveal truth by selfless service, shall the next revelation unfold. It is fast coming as inspiration to receptive, All-centered souls.

"Keep on tuning in, Mom, and do not let merely logical or scientific attitudes retard your awareness of this inflow of Light. It is not an inflow into the mind, but into the spirit which controls the mind's radio. Read and study all you can; yes, that is the way to increase the receptivity of the mind. It does not make the mind infallible, but it does make it more capable of absorption of eternal values.

"As you increasingly dwell in spirit atmosphere, as you seek more of Light, your personal vibration will be raised to a higher level. This does not mean any abnormal way of living; it means the whole of living will be stepped up. You will have better health, better balance, more laughter, more understanding and more tolerance. Light is pouring in. When man asks for Light, there are thousands of souls here rejoicing and waiting to help. We can do nothing unless you ask. That is the law. Development is each man's personal acceptance of the Light. God gave man free will, for He is Love. The wider one opens the door to Love, the more inclusive that love becomes; the more one puts the good of others first, the more does Light release, and freedom infuse that one with triumph.

"Man cannot wish the dark away,
Nor wishing bring the light of day.
'Tis bidding self be mutely still
And linking self with God's own will
That turns the darkness into Light,
Revealing Truth to man's dim sight."

28

PRAISE AND GRATITUDE

The next message came at a time of difficult personal adjustment. We were living in Washington until time to go to Maine again in the spring. The hectic city life was confusing after the peace and quiet of our months in Maine and after our years of living in a small town, and I am afraid I fell prey to the subtle temptation of discouragement. I was aware that I was not living up to the best I knew and that I was not following the excellent advice I had received from Lowell and other spirits. Distracted by temporary problems, I had lost some of my peace of mind and some of my sense of direction. The disappointment of each failure seemed to intensify the fog separating me from the world of spirit, the world of light and joy.

I realize that I am attempting to describe an experience familiar to many, a painful period of seeming stagnation, a spiritual low point. All who are struggling to follow the upward path must meet similar testing and training. We all have special weaknesses and blind spots, and to each of us come days in the valley when the mountain top becomes obscure and all-too-dim a memory. Sooner or later we discover, or recall, the magic lifting qualities of praise and gratitude. On this gloomy November day, Lowell reminds me of those two positive and powerful means of assistance, and his words were responsible in large part for a reversal in my thinking and in my attitude. Gradually I began to feel more "in tune" spiritually and to be more aware of Lowell and help from the other side.

Washington, D. C.
November 11, 1946

"Mom, Mom, Mom, I know your heart has been heavy these past few days. I am always within reach when your cry is for the awakening of mankind, but when you are cluttered with self-confusion and self-adjustment to mere temporary problems, I fade from your consciousness.

"You have been in a fog. Your eyes have been shut to light and joy. I have no power in this fog. It is you who must bid it disperse that the true course of your life may be more visible. Time is short on earth, and there is much you are bidden to do. You must not lose your perspective while on the turning, twisting road ahead of you. You have allowed your gift of sensitivity to be lessened by mass vibrations. There is a real purpose in your being where you are. You can and must learn to shut off the thoughts of others even in the roaring traffic of a muddled city. Until you do this, you will be like a budding flower, too weak to withstand the winds of frustration. It is the roots of the flowering which bring the strength, not the blossoming. A flowering heart naturally turns toward the light but, if its roots are not secure and nourished, it will droop and fade. Feed your roots with gratitude until the tiny tendrils take stronger fastenings in the soil. Your roots are your soul's growth within. Gratitude and praise will devitalize frustrations. The desire to lay blossoms of deeds and thoughts on the altar of God is not enough. You must also make your flowering stronger, more beautiful, more life-filled. It is easy to thrive in a sheltered garden, but you are asked to flourish in more difficult surroundings. It is all part of your

training. Keep on trying—not with self-will, but with joy and gratitude.

"*First, you must concentrate on that which you have started. Select your place of writing. Bid us who yearn to help you to meet you there each day. Put this above all other duties. When you show determined and concentrated effort, invisible forces will rally to direct and aid you. It is not they, but you, who have cut off guidance and inspiration. You must vibrate to joy before you can express the messages we are ready to send through you. Earth souls need joy rather than mere happiness. Happiness springs from the material, but joy is purely spiritual. Joy bubbles from within, and no man can take it away. Happiness comes from without, and man can destroy its fickle abidings with thoughts as well as with actions. Be not as a candle whose glow comes from a slender wick and is at the mercy of every passing breath. Be as a steady electric light which brings vision as long as the current flows from the power-house. Stand firm, Mom, we need your attunement more than you realize. Peace and joy cannot be permanent in your heart until it responds to that work allotted to you alone. We here love you and pour out to you fresh supplies of energy and joy which we hope you will use in the right way. Concentration and consecration are the springboards of power.*"

29

A BIT OF EVIDENTIAL

Reading over the messages of this period, I see clearly that, as always, Lowell was steadfastly trying to help and lift me. The next message provides an excellent example of his patience, of his infinitely more mature spiritual outlook, of his ever-present concern in helping me to help others and of his persuasiveness in leading me toward fuller acceptance of truth-thoughts. Nevertheless, the pull of this world and its mass thinking exert a strong influence. Not content with other-worldly assistance and understanding alone, I craved earthly reinforcement.

That fall I had heard of a highly respected spiritualist minister named Mrs. Young* and had a strong desire to see her, with the hope that she would in some way substantiate my own experiences in psychic matters. Meeting me at my stage of development, Lowell apparently decided to humor me in my desire for proof and therefore influenced me to see Mrs. Young. Appropriately, Lowell did not merely satisfy my personal longing but used the experience to relay his son's message to our friend, Marvin*. Also, the occasion enabled Lowell to emphasize thoughts of universal scope.

During my visit with Mrs. Young, she said,

"Your boy is bringing a young man who went out of this life very suddenly. Do you know whom I mean?"

I was baffled as to the identity of the young man until

---

* See Preface.

Mrs. Young told me the name of his home town, many miles from Washington. Whereupon I realized he must be Marvin's son who had recently been killed in a plane accident. Deeply impressed by this unexpected happening, I was even more affected when Lowell's message the next morning proved to be an interpretive sequel to the day before. As to Lowell's verifying of my identification of Marvin's son, that did not surprise me and seemed only natural.

The culmination of the story is that Marvin unexpectedly came to see us a few months later. Obviously I had no choice but to read him the following message and parts of a later one concerning him in an attempt to stimulate his interest in the continuity of life and in the need for releasing our loved ones.

Washington, D. C.
November 25, 1946

"Dear Mom, I heard your plea in church for clearer understanding about our talks with each other. Like other earth-souls you react waveringly instead of accepting the clearly defined pathway ahead of you. I urged you to see Mrs. Young. It was not that she could do anything for you which you cannot do better for yourself; it was to give you a bit of proof, for which you are still asking. Obedience to persistent urges, even though you think them strange, develops your awareness to psychic force. As I have told you over and over, doubt, uncertainty and too much rationalizing hinder the development of such a gift. Does a musician analyze the flashes of inspiration which come to him when he is expressing the beauty of harmony? Does an artist ponder why the flashes of color come to his inner eye and enable him to reproduce them in a material form? Does an inspired preacher stop to examine the words of truth

*when he is moved to express the mind of creative force?
Never! That way all would be mediocre and unconvincing.
One must be abandoned to that which one believes in
order to be a channel of inspiration.*

*"As your subconscious or creative mind is unfettered and
freed to relay thoughts, so will your conscious mind improve in its capacity to grow and absorb. One reacts on
the other; where there is growth and enlightenment of one,
there is a similar process in the other. In the same way,
one cannot grow spiritually without refreshing and aug-
menting physical and mental capacities.*

*"You will see Marvin, so please tell him his son is alive
and striving to understand what has happened to him.
His birth into this plane was so sudden that he is bewildered. He longs to reach the minds of his loved ones on
earth, but there is a curtain of doubt delaying him. Tell
Marvin sometime (you will have the opportunity) that
mere resignation is not enough to free his son. Marvin must
regard his son's passing not as a trick of fate, not as a great
tragedy, but as a glorious mission into eternity. There must
be joy for him and a releasing of pondering and grief before he will be completely awakened to reality. The son
asked last night for my help in reaching his family. I am
depending on your understanding and love to open the
door for him. As his numbness begins to wear off, he longs
for his family to understand. His children never question
his nearness. They are wiser in the laws of eternity than the
older members of the family.*

*"Nothing can stop the purposes of the Creator. Man was
created 'in His image.' This law is beyond human comprehension, but men take it too literally. 'His image' is the reflection of All-Perfection in each human soul; therefore, all
growth comes through desire for perfection. Whatsoever*

man desires is either the deterring or the motivating force for development of his own soul. What you call death is often the awakening of an intensified desire to learn the laws which govern a soul's evolvement toward the Creator's majesty.

"Here, we still have freedom to choose whether we will help the whole race in its march of evolution or whether we will cling to personal desires. Those on earth who are releasing their departed ones have a greater influence than they know in helping those here to orient themselves in their decisions. Many souls on this plane are confused, retarded, or even made instruments of evil because earth minds, in their blind ignorance, are holding them in bondage. What we aim to implant into your mind is that you have the privilege of stressing to others that there is no death except when man puts his human desires before the purposes of God."

30

THE ABYSS OF TIME

Although the next writing is not from Lowell, it is included here because it seems to continue the train of thought begun by him four days earlier. It is one of many I have found which were written while we were in Washington that winter. This one happens to have been written after prayer or a "quiet time" with our friend, Grace Helen Earle. For many years now she and her husband have been closely associated with us in healing work, prayer groups and a rewarding spiritual fellowship.

I bring out this fact to illustrate a pertinent truth about prayer and fellowship—the power of being in accord with like-minded souls. The familiar Pentecostal words, "they were with one accord in one place," are to the point here. "In accord" implies first and foremostly a deep-level oneness in Christ, but it may also include agreement on specific needs brought to God in intercessory or personal prayer. "If two of you shall agree on earth as touching anything that they shall ask, it shall be done for them of my Father which is in Heaven." In this experience of Grace Helen and myself, I believe the meeting of our spirits helped create an atmosphere of soul peace. Wordlessly we thanked God that He had heard and answered us. Then unexpectedly the following message came in the silence. It seemed an attempt to express, if only in part, our thoughts and feelings "too deep for words."

Washington, D. C.
November 29, 1946

"*Into the abyss of time, reflected in the mirror of space, come the thoughts of all mankind, to build the mansions of eternity. Thoughts are the fabric from which dreams are made so that consecrated workmen may bring about their manifestations.*

"*All creation sings its song of perfection, the perfect dream thought of the Creator. It is complete, timeless, endless, a preconceived vision of unearthly loveliness. It stands like a dazzling beacon light whose rays forever permeate into the consciousness of men, urging them by silent tuggings within to re-create that which is already perfect in timeless mind.*

"*Too often the creative flow in man's mind is reversed. It should flow from the great river of fullness and beauty toward the finite mind, instead of from his own limited mind toward that universal center of creation. Men are capable of receiving but a mere fraction of the available inflow if they wrongly use their own minds as its origin.*

"*The culmination of human attainment is the expression of belief in the Creator's purposes. The ideal fixation is a constant, earnest desire to be capable of receiving from divine mind. Man is meant to express the essence of God-promptings. Therefore, no great creative spirit on earth can produce masterpieces of expression unless his finite mind is stilled and secondary to the Great Mind. No person can develop the potential beauty of his own soul expression in any other way.*

"*Man must make himself more flexible to the creative urge by cleansing discordant whimperings of the self-mind. Cloudiness, conflict, ceaseless striving—all these must go before real truths can flow uninterruptedly. Perfect peace*

*must spring from its own source to quiet every nerve, per-
plexity, and outworn conception.*

*"You ask why this peace is so fleeting, so illusive. It is
because problems are given a more prominent place than
God in your minds. Dwell above earthly problems and
worldly conflicts. Breathe in peace of mind as a child
breathes in the fresh, pure air. Musty cells will be cleansed,
refreshed and stimulated by dwelling in the peace vibration.
In accord with the receptivity of your conscious mind shall
be your awareness of that great inflow which is ever waiting
to enter your soul-minds."*

31

LOVE AND LIGHT

This chapter contains a sample of many personal training messages which continued to urge me on to a more selfless life. Often repeated was the emphasis on grateful, even joyous, overcoming of weakness and trials so that I could become a more effective channel for "love and light." These lessons had to be repeated because numerous mistakes were made. Again I am astounded at how apparently little I heeded or appreciated the help and encouragement given to me. Yet, "all things are possible with God." Spiritual growth advances, often in a way and at a pace comprehended by neither ourselves nor our world, but only by Him whose patience and insight are infinitely tender and all-seeing. His Grace leads each of us who truly seeks Him. Always are there new challenges, but always are His Love and Strength superbly sufficient.

Washington, D. C.
December 1, 1946

"You are too eager to see and do instead of being merely a channel lighted with love. You must love not only people but everything, material or spiritual, which helps you to see the Light more clearly. Love and Light are one; one cannot thrive without the other. Where Light is, darkness cannot be; where Love is, discord cannot be. Therefore, if you would have peace, love all life—even its failures, its frustrations and its sufferings, for Love lifts every experience above that which it seems to be up into clear triumphancy.

"It is not what happens to a human that counts; it is his ability to face and rise above any experience, thus putting himself in tune with eternal values rather than with earthly problems.

"One who does not grow through his earthly experiences is already dead. He is living in his own dream world, far from Reality. Until his attitude changes, until he accepts life's rebuffs as tools to sharpen his growth, his soul is stunted. Hence, he is dead to life's Truth. Blessed indeed is he who can stumble and fall to rise again and say 'thank you' for chances to learn. Blessed is he who meets every closed door and every challenge with a grateful heart, knowing that these are opportunities leading him to greater wisdom. Life's lessons must be learned; they will reappear again and again, in one form or another, until the self-soul faces them and conquers them. One may dawdle on the way, one may rationalize, one may refuse to face earth lessons, but some day they must be mastered; this is the law of being. Therefore, learn quickly the lessons which are given to you. Love them and be grateful for them, for love opens the way to light. When love and light dwell in a human heart, there are found the abundance, the beauty and the joy of timelessness."

32

THE THREE WISE MEN

The following message about the Three Wise Men is an example of writing which came to me at a time when I was especially uplifted. This was a glorious Christmas Day, and our Saviour seemed to rejoice with us; His Love was indeed triumphant.

We were also happily aware that Junie was to be married the following afternoon to his lovely Jean. Unhappily, the next morning I was to fall from joyous heights to discouraging depths. I mention here these sharply contrasting emotions on Junie's wedding day because they illustrate an ever-present danger. When we reach a high point in spiritual life we are apt, unwittingly, to admit the old self in some form, often that of spiritual pride. We are so happy, life is so wonderful and never again will we slip back into our old selves! We may not think all this consciously but, unless we are on guard, our dependence on God alone may falter.

However, the wonder of God's way is that no matter how far we slip, we will not be lost if we call on Him. He will lift us out of any pit into which we have fallen. He will set our feet once more on the right path, even as were those of the Wise Men again and again returned to the following of the Star and its vision.

Washington, D. C.
December 25, 1946

"The Three Wise Men were the forerunners of the har-

mony of the universe. With inner eyes they beheld the vision of peace on earth. Their hard, weary way to the call from Cosmic Light was beset with doubt and even unbelief. Attuned to vibrations of unseen power, they came to earth. Their hearts were alight with visions even though their pondering minds could not fathom their significance. Their magnetic, intuitive urge to reach the Light was more un-yielding than the limitations and doubts of earth time. So they traveled on, bearing their gifts to Bethlehem, seeing with inner eyes the purposes of time. The little babe they found was almost an anticlimax to their confused reason-ing. Yet their destiny was fulfilled. They pointed the way to the seed-light whose power was to unfold for years and years until it would finally vitalize the whole earth.

"Slowly against barriers of man's dampened hopes has the seed pulsated with life. It has grown stronger, more intense and nearer the ultimate vision. Against the hard clay of hate, against the rain of tears from frustrated ideals, the seed has prevailed. Against the scorching sun—burning skepticism and doubt—against the cold night—selfishness and greed—against storms of war and destruction, against all neglect, has the tiny light-seed prevailed. It is driven ever onward by the force of eternal life.

"Today that dream vision of the Three Wise Men is reaching into all the earth as never before. Time is ripe for the unfoldment of the ultimate glory of the seed of truth. It is to the wise men of today, whose vision is attuned to greet it, that revelations are pouring in to transform the drab, material world into the timeless world of spirit. Their eyes are fastened in expectancy upon the released power of perfection. They will see the star as clearly as the Three Wise Men of ancient time. They will see the first signs of *triumphant majesty as the cosmic power is made manifest and the forces of darkness cringe and retreat.*

"Greet this new day with joyful praise, ye wise ones of today; lift your eyes and behold the star of peace approaching on wings of lighted silence. The song of the angels is breaking through; their anthems of joy reverberate in the ears of the wise ones. Listen this Christmas time to its ethereal melody. The love and prayers of all the wise ones are attuned to the anthem of eternal harmony.

"The tiny life-seed is bursting its bonds of materialism which have too long retarded it. Matured and released, it is power, beauty and love. The ripening time is here; the harvest is ready. Watch for the new star, ye wise ones. On its ray will the Prince of Peace descend in power and glory upon this earth to rule supreme in the hearts of men. Be prepared to receive Him. He will come sooner than you think. Ye wise ones, the lights you carry soon will be merged with All-Light. Then shall you behold the glorified promise of 'Peace on earth, good will to all men.'"

33

SELF STEPS IN

December 26, 1946, was Junie's wedding day and I awoke that morning with a glad and delighted heart because of Junie and Jean. Suddenly, I felt Lowell's bright presence in the room. He radiated happiness and obviously was sharing and participating in the joy of the day. Unfortunately, the living force of Lowell's personality had the wrong effect on me and, at that moment, I fell far from the heights of yesterday's Christmas joy. With consternation and with incredulity at my own emotions, I felt my peace and happiness abruptly disappear. Instead of rejoicing with him, I was inexplicably thrown back to a violent mother-longing for my son. Yearning possessed me, yearning for the impossible, for Lowell's wedding day, for a son's wife to love, and yes, even for my never-to-be-born grandchildren.

Some vulnerable spot in my spiritual armor had allowed Lowell's nearness to arouse such strong human longings that my usual spirit-awareness was obliterated for the time being. Not even feeling as if I could attend the wedding, I battled with myself and my confused emotions for several hours. Deeply concerned, Franklin tried to help me and to reason with me. When we could become quiet, we had a prayer together; that and the following message were instrumental in restoring me.

Washington, D. C.
December 26, 1946

*"Mom, dearest Mom, this is Junie's wedding day, and
we three surely want him to be happy. I love you all, and
I am sorry I have upset you. All this emotion will fade.
Everything on earth will pass away, but love never will. I
know your heart longings; no one else can understand how
hard you have tried to put earth love for me out of your
heart and to replace it with universal love. I know the fight
in your soul to be bigger than you are, but you must let
me in today. Please don't crowd me out. All should be joy,
but I feel your heart heavy unto bursting with unfulfilled
human dreams. You can not expect others to understand.*

*"Just keep steady, and you will not fail. Your bitter cup
must become a fresh draught of life and joy; you must not
let anything unsweeten it again.*

*"Each soul has a fight, but you must forget yours today.
I know you do not want to hurt Dad. We three are eternally
linked by a love deeper than torrents of human emotion.
The Christ-in-us bids us forget self to serve Him, and Him
alone.*

*"I shall be nearer than your breathing today, nearer
than your fondest dream. Together we shall conquer, we
shall not fail. Failure means separation and, where Christ's
love is burning, there is no separation. Let's have fun today.
Please be gay, Mom, and all shadows will flee. I like your
new hat, but I would like to see a smile beneath it, a warm,
joyous smile. All is well, but time and opportunity are
quickly passing. Rejoice and be exceeding glad, for the reward is greater than human understanding. Keep steady—
I love you—I am trying to enter in to sing in your heart."*

My recovery was amazingly complete; soon no trace of

anguish remained. Later I cheerfully dressed for the cere-
mony and, with tender amusement, put on the new hat
which Lowell had admired. We thoroughly enjoyed the
wedding and the reception just as we had been anticipating.
We loved Junie dearly, we were pleased in every way about
his lovely bride, and their wedding is now one of our most
pleasant memories. With a gratefully warm heart, I sensed
that Lowell was there with us all; in fact, he seemed to
stand behind Junie and Jean like a golden light full of rich
blessing. I could almost see him in that light, and my whole
soul responded to his joy, which I realized was intensified
by my earlier victory over self-longings.

A few years before, Lowell had suggested that Junie "put
his dreams in a tightly closed box." We recalled those pic-
turesque words on his wedding day and were contentedly
aware that their implied promise seemed to be coming true.
Junie had grown into a fine young man of whom we were
very proud and, in the intervening years, he has continued
to be happily successful in his career and in the larger areas
of life.

Warmly responsive, full of loving charm, unusually capable, Jean is a combination of all that we ever dreamed a
daughter could be, and in their five children we have found
our ideal grandchildren. We sincerely feel as close to Junie
and Jean as if they were our own children and, of course,
much happiness has come to us through our deep affection
for all seven of "our family." Instinctively, we know that
Lowell delights in this loving relationship and that he is a
vital part of the unusually strong bond between us.

Without question, this chapter's message is one which
came in answer to a definite need. In the morning Lowell
had come to me, just as an earthly son might have, to talk
over an exciting day. It was almost as if he had said,

"Oh, Mom, isn't it grand for Junie and Jean?"

When I reacted selfishly to my vivid awareness of him, he then tried to rescue me from my dark mood and to lift me to my better self, which recognizes that Lowell is now more alive than ever.

34

ACROSS THE CHASM

Lowell speaks in the following writing of my dream the preceding night. All I could recall of it the next day was hauntingly beautiful music such as I had never heard or even imagined. It was almost as if I had been with a heavenly host and caught its rapturous joy. The celestial harmony of angels echoed gloriously in my dream and carried over into the morning so realistically that it was with me all day. The dream-remembered phrase, "I am the whole universe," kept singing within me; in fact, my blood seemed to be pulsing to its rhythm. Frequently that day I could not resist singing aloud the fragmentary words and melody. Vainly I tried to recapture the entire beauty of the words and music, but only the one line, "I am the whole universe," came clearly. The rest remained a vague, heaven-toned sensation of harmony. Neither could I fathom the depth of meaning in "I am the whole universe." I knew it was a theme song and that Lowell was part of its symphony. Did it mean that Lowell was now nearer to Reality and to the great Oneness of the universe? The thought came to me that joy and adoration are all that is or ever will be. Joy and adoration for the Holy Trinity are Eternity, are the ultimate for every soul.

With my heart pounding, I wondered why this touch of divine joy had been given to me. However, I knew then and I know more surely now that too much conjecturing about reasons is never wise. I can only add that this day stands out as one of profound meaning and of unusual oneness with Lowell, with the next world and, above all, with Him Who is the Lord and Master of all worlds without end. A mountain top experience, the ecstasy and revelation came unsought, undeserved and in the abundance which is His alone to give.

The most gratifying thought of all was that divine contact and awareness are always possible for every one of us who chooses the Christ-Way. In contrast, Lowell often reminds us of the encroachment of evil and that, without God, each of us is susceptible to all error and sin. When we turn to Him and His overflowing Goodness, "Eye hath not seen, nor ear heard, nor have entered into the hearts of man, the things that God hath prepared for them that love Him."

Since I was writing poetry in those days, I decided that the words, "I am the whole universe," were intended for me to use as a theme for a poem. Accordingly, I attempted to describe the indescribable in poetry, but various interruptions and the fact that we must attend a funeral that afternoon contributed to my lack of success. The results were merely a few incomplete and quite unsatisfactory lines of verse. Apparently verse was not the right medium, but the following message significantly expresses, at least in part, the theme suggested in my dream.

The funeral we were attending was held in Arlington Chapel and was that of a close friend in the Navy. It was a very large service with countless flowers, many candles and movingly appropriate music. Leaving the chapel, we decided to stop at Lowell's grave for a moment of prayer. We seldom visited the spot because of our sure knowledge that Lowell is spirit and that, as such, he most certainly is not confined there or in any one place. Being so near, however, it seemed natural to pause there, and we were rewarded by the warmth and joy which filled us.

As we entered our car to drive home, a desire to write came to me suddenly and powerfully. No paper appeared to be available but, as the impulse grew increasingly strong, I insisted we find something. All we could collect were some old envelopes and scraps of paper, and I even used margins of the day's newspaper. Franklin says he will never forget either my sense of urgency or the rapidity with which I covered all usable paper with this message on death.

Washington, D. C.
January 26, 1947

"Mom, Mom:

"I am not there in that grave, for I am everywhere. You do not know my joy, nor my scattering into eternity, but you feel it.

"You heard our anthem of praise last night in your dream, but you remember only one running theme, 'I am the whole universe.' What you felt on awakening was the first vibratory tone of joy, a complete joy such as man never knows on earth. He receives only faint reverberations of the lower tones. Heavenly joy is music which human ears cannot record, although the inner-soul-ears catch a beat now and then.

"You saw death and felt his chill blackness as he rode on earth today to claim his own. Your penetration went with him across the chasms of the unknown into the portals of universal existence. I heard you tell Dad what you sensed, but it was really I speaking in your mind. I am continually trying to infuse into your earth mind the oneness of all creation and the immensity of life as it flows from countless planes back and forth, shining like the fire-gold of sunsets.

"No one has looked upon the face of death, for hidden beneath his black robes, which are but the symbols of earth blindness, is that which man can not gaze upon. When death bears his precious burden from the black despair of earth, he swiftly crosses the chasm which divides time and eternity. As he approaches the unknown areas of endless vitality, he throws off the shadowy garments or, rather, the garments fall away as if they had never existed. Then death is revealed as the angel of light with such radiance that the new-born eyes open for the first time. Earth-bound souls cannot stand the light and close their eyes, preferring to sleep. The shock is too great for their senses. Some sleep for a few hours, some for years and there are some who sleep for centuries.

"But to those who believe in the continuity of life and to those who have served the greater urges of life, the light of death falls like a blessing. From the great illumination in the face of the angel of death comes the sensation of ethereal, shifting, flowing colors, like a rainbow in whirling motion. These indescribable colors, taking vaporous form, gradually settle into familiar things. The new soul looks with surprise upon his own body which is burning with the intensity of a silver-infused flame. I should like to be able to tell you so that your human conception of color can be stepped up to eternal color. Do you remember the flowers on the altar, and in the chapel, today at the funeral services? Could you, in your imagination, dip each color of each separate flower into the silver-gold flame of the altar candles and then set it whirling and leaping until it flowed like the organ vibration? This is a little like the sight which greets the eyes of the one who has crossed over. From out of this color-blended light, this vital substance, are formed the new bodies of the living dead.

"*These luminous bodies flow with ecstasy into the bodies
of their loved ones who are waiting to greet them. The
impact causes vibrations of such intense wonderment and
joy that it is akin to earth symphonies magnified a hundred
thousand times. They are one with its unearthly harmony
and find themselves moving to the beat of its insistent
cadences; at first slowly, then more swiftly and trium-
phantly, these souls begin to see death in its reality.*

"*Death is but release from earth limitations and earth
conceptions. It is a new life which knows no time, space
nor distance. Its momentum is the blending of the vibrations of color and music. Its gardens are opportunity for
service. Here we are aware of the tools which can be used
to sharpen our minds for keener penetration into the purposes of our Creator.*

"*We can choose and work out our own plan for further
ventures toward the Light of all Lights. Our interpenetrating senses give us greater wisdom.*

"*Almost every forward-going soul chooses that which he
is best fitted to do, often going right on with the same work
he did on earth. The very assuring part of death is its
naturalness. What is more natural than to go to bed at
night, to sleep soundly, to awaken refreshed and ready for
the day's task? What is more natural than to sleep for a
while in the arms of death and to awaken to a new day
refreshed and vitally equipped to go on with the larger
work?*

"*I am allowed to tell you all this, Mom, that in your
writings you will carry to the readers the hope of the indescribable joy that is to come to all awakened souls when
they pass over. You must let them know that earth is but
a training school to improve latent faculties and to put into
action soul-desires, which are the motivating force of exis-*

tence. Men should and must love earth living but, even more, they should love its opportunities for learning and lifting others to higher levels.

"The blind, unawakened, selfish ones not only are marking time with stagnation, but they are also making it difficult for us to use our higher knowledge. Earth must wake up and grasp the significance of your dream song, 'I am the Whole Universe.'"

35

FREEING OUR LOVED ONES

Consciously trying to write and to ask for only the highest truth, I began to feel more sense of direction behind my messages as well as a keener awareness of the next plane. It was gratifying to have Lowell begin the next message by thanking me for my co-operation with the invisible world.

We are here given tangible evidence of the need for releasing our loved ones by relinquishing human longing to accept the larger or eternal point of view. Our self-centered emotions hold back those who have passed on from fulfilling their destinies. Furthermore, this limiting attitude retards our own spiritual growth. The continuity of life is a two-way affair. Those on the other side need our help, understanding and prayer just as we need theirs. We must, therefore, strive to keep the channels of love between the two worlds free from the blockage of doubt or self and, thus, ever receptive to the flow of truth and light.

This message came the night before our friend, Marvin*, the man whose son had been killed in a plane crash a few months earlier, came to see us.

Washington, D. C.
February 18, 1947

"Thank you for your co-operation, Mom. My work is now reaching out to new strata and is more effective as I

---

* See Preface.

develop through research and absorption of truth. This does not mean that I am growing away from you, but it does mean that your growth must keep pace with mine to maintain a vital and receptive communication.

"You sometimes feel these messages are becoming more abstract. Why shouldn't they? Your personal life has become, perhaps without your being aware of it, more of a universal one. You asked to serve in the highest way possible, you reached out for that life, then you wonder why it comes in a seemingly impersonal way. You still unconsciously yearn for more proof. You are not meant, on your plane, to have more proof. Sometimes it comes sublimated in truth. Your whole purpose in writing is to relay, by a desire-infused receptivity, such truths as your subconscious mind can absorb from higher planes of thought. Should you use this gift primarily to obtain proof or to command acclaim, then it would be withdrawn.

"This sensitivity entrusted to you must be guarded, cherished and often sublimated into impersonal truths. There are many reasons why I should not, even if I wished, reveal personal, evidential facts. First of all, these facts, seemingly very vital to you, are really of minor importance. Secondly, human situations are changeable and not powerful enough to get through as clearly as the universal truths.

"The messages which do get through are permanent, indestructible patterns. Each is separately and minutely attuned to each earth-channel. Thus, universal thought-patterns are given to be re-expressed in one's own way. Love and desire to serve unselfish purposes make one aware of this inflow. Many souls have the receptivity but have never made the outreaching connection because of their lack of faith in things unseen or their lack of desire to do invisible research.

"Much harm has been done our cause of inter-plane communication by receptive souls who have received wisdom but have re-expressed it for personal gain or on the level of human interpretation only. These unconsecrated souls are bringing the truths, which are ever unfolding on this plane, down to the level of the shifting and limited earth expression. It just cannot be done that way. We here, who are co-operating with all-existence, are not at liberty to pamper earth questioners by revealing earth solutions to earth problems, except when it will increase susceptibility to our higher state of living. Many need help in comprehending that life goes on continually and ever more abundantly. You do not need evidential messages to prove this. Your very life should reflect it, should be contagious to those who are seeking to know; furthermore, unless others are truly seeking, all your efforts will fall on barren ground.

"Often as earth life progresses toward preparation for change, the desire for illumination grows in proportion. A great truth we learn on earth is the realization that we do not possess our possessions. They often possess us, but we never possess them. They are loaned to us and are of permanent use only when we relinquish them and share them with those whose need is greater than our own. Then they become blessings.

"The more you on earth believe in immortality, the more will the value of material things shrink. The freer man is from claims of materiality and from possessiveness of all things feeding self-importance, the freer is he to receive and find joy in the real, eternal things.

"When a man doubts the reality of life continuous-after-death, he naturally centers his belief in things temporal and seen. When these all pass, often in the twinkling of an eye, too late he realizes the time he has wasted and his adjust-

ment to this next phase of living is more difficult. Such an
unawakened soul in your world retards the growth and
usefulness of his loved ones here who are trying to disentangle themselves from the magnetic downpull of their
earth ones. Men must some way be made to realize their
responsibility toward their released ones. It is vital to keep
the door of belief open that the purposes of existence may
be communicated. This is your purpose, Mom, to help open
the doors to our plane that those here will not feel isolated
nor those on earth forsaken.

"Do not worry that you cannot prove your confident
belief, just go on believing, trusting and co-operating; then
will your spirit permeate the darkness of unbelieving minds.
It will give them the incentive to reach out beyond human
existence into reality. Once man reaches out, his faith will
be increased, material values will be put in their right perspective and heart-consciousness will expand as naturally as
a flower opens to the sun.

"Remember when you talk to Marvin that you are not
only hoping to increase his belief in survival of personality
but also to help him sense the power, peace and usefulness
emanating from true faith. One may know in one's mind,
but such knowledge must be in one's heart before it will
grow and flourish and open new vistas. Marvin's son has
work to do, greater work than he could have accomplished
on the earth plane. However, he must be released by loving
earth ones before he can fully concentrate and be receptive
to the training which will speed his ascension toward the
Light. He sends love and thanks to all his dear ones; his
sight is refreshed, and boundless energy waits to lead him
to greater accomplishments. He speaks often into the heart-
minds of his wife and children. They must think of him as a
guardian angel, ever loving and ever hovering to direct

their impulses into the lighted way. Only their doubt shuts him out and confuses him. They must let him into their lives, grateful for his desire to be the joy-shadow in their earth darkness.

"You and I, Mom, are so united in purpose that nothing can separate us. Our desire is to live life to its fullest, now and forever, and to share this fullness wherever lack of truth has tarnished life's brightness."

36

COSMIC ADVENTURING

The following two messages continue the theme of the oneness of all life and of the always present opportunity to link our finite selves with God's great creative oneness. Only thus do we become partakers of our rightful and glorious heritage.

Sebasco Estates, Maine
May 27, 1947

"Forces are gathering for an experiment in cosmic communication. Tune in and fix your mind on the immensity, the grandeur, the everlastingness of the universe. Forget, as far as possible, the laws of the earth planet. See the great cosmic laws as the center of all-consciousness, ever governing the multitude of lesser laws.

"Man's world is like something seen through the wrong end of a telescope. Everything is diminutive, petty, out of true perspective. From the other end is seen the real universe existing in minute detail of law and order, yet too out of reach for man to fathom. Just as science is advancing rapidly in many ways by its power to look through the telescope, so must man's thinking advance through his ability to contact the spiritual as well as the material aspects of the universe.

"Today detach your consciousness from every preconceived idea. Think of your self as spirit, as a part of the whole of creation, not as an individual limited by the laws

of gravitation and habits of thinking. You will be free in as much as you forget limitations and rise to the higher vibrations of cosmic consciousness. Turn your mental telescope the right way around and see the whole of life in its true light.

"Creation is still creating. It goes on forever. As in mathematical law, mind is relating its various potentialities to the potentialities of perfection. Every phase of nature is creating toward its ultimate perfection, which exists like a seed of intelligence and must express itself according to its destiny. Every form of life, animate or seemingly inanimate, is responding to the laws of the cosmic urge. There are periods of inactivity and periods of stimulation, some lasting a second, some a million or more years. Yet evolution moves onward.

"Even the suns of the universe are changing and re-creating their force as a means of relaying life-essence.

"In life there is no beginning and no ending. Think of the immensity and complexity of the mind-intelligence which ever was and ever is and which is moving in mysterious ways to bring to perfection all of life. You are part of this. Your nature is inseparable from its power. Let your mind practice thinking of the flow to earth center from the center of all-intelligence. Catch the rhythm of such an adventure. The kernel of your consciousness buried by ages of mass, self-centered thought is forever free to compensate for limitations by absorbing and being absorbed in super-consciousness.

"Your first lesson in cosmic adventuring is to realize the greatness of the opportunity offered man. He may choose to be either man of clay with self-reflected areas of wisdom or man nourished and inspired by conscious union with the supreme force. When Christ said, 'I and my Father are *one,' He meant I, the permanent spark of divine essence living as mere man, can outstrip the limitations of the flesh and abide in the consciousness of all-perfection. He used the word 'Father' because it is the symbol of family authority. He had to use words so simple yet so universal and eternal that they would be guiding principles not only for the simple fishermen and the partially illiterate masses of His day but also for the scholars of our age and all ages to come. Often the simple man sees quickly and grasps the hidden laws, whereas the scholar misses their point because he is so filled with his own learning and theories that he is blinded. One must become as a little child. Intelligence is an unbalancing force unless it is linked with heart-knowing. To know with the mind is excellent; to know with the heart is an asset transcending any other knowledge. To know with the mind and to harmonize this knowing with the heart is a combination which will overcome any obstacle and will lead on to victory—mental, spiritual and physical.*

"*Knowledge unused is wasted. It must have a focused sense of direction and must be used for a purpose to be of any value; wisdom heard in the heart and not obeyed is useless. It merely confuses, like listening to two masters; however, wisdom and knowledge working in harmony are an invincible combination.*

"*Therefore, you who seek knowledge, what would you do with it? You who seek wisdom, where would you employ it? You who strive for knowledge combined with heart-wisdom, where will you direct your energy and power? You must have a mark. If it is for self, you will be no bigger than the self-mind; if it is for others, you will be a comforter and peace-maker on earth; but, if it is toward the creative oneness of all consciousness, toward linking yourself with all-perfection, then will you tune in to the great cosmic laws and be a participant in the continuing process of creation. You will be a part of cosmic law and entrusted with its truths. You will be inspiration for lesser developed souls. You will be joy and light shining in the reflected glory of the great Light. So, I say, aim high. Think in terms of allness, of eternal time, of unlimited space, of unforgettable joy."*

Sebasco Estates, Maine
July 4, 1947

"There is always a message, always a song in each minute of eternity. When mind, heart and ears are attuned, the echo is heard clearly as you listen. Think of each moment of this day as a means of attunement to this perfection. Do not let the static of the divided mind mar the beauty which is yours for the asking. Peace and joy are ever singing through the ether; would you give them free rein in yourself or would you curb them with the capricious waves of inharmony which are hovering about your earth consciousness? Choose for yourself and command the minutes as you command the turning of a radio dial.

"Eternity is now, this very second. Earth experiences are shifting and unreal; therefore, fortify yourself with the feeling of foreverness. Attach your thinking to those things which are changeless and you will always have the song of the minutes in your heart. Love is lasting, love is the essence of all timelessness."

37

TEARING DOWN WALLS

September 22nd is the date when Lowell left us. Eleven years later, back in Maine again on that date, I hoped for a personal word from him. The following message is the result. I knew, of course, that Lowell was spirit, but I was too apt to think of spirit in cold and nebulous form. In this message Lowell comforts my mother-heart and goes on to emphasize the survival of personality as well as to assure me of the warmth and naturalness of spirit.

Lowell here helps clarify my thinking on some of my personal problems, especially those concerning intuitive ability. I had weakened this gift by too frequently allowing people and outward conditions to upset my balance and inner poise. One of my major difficulties has always been to find and to live according to the rhythm right for me alone. So many times I have thought I had to keep up with what the world expected or with what my friends were doing. The unpleasant result would be bewilderment and a sense of inadequacy followed by exhaustion. I have been slow in learning the lessons necessary for overcoming this personality-block to soul growth, and I well realize that its threat is still present.

On the more positive side, I can now see that my perception and my belief in myself as a child of God were strengthening over the years. Increasingly strong, too, was the realization that extrasensory gifts do not come by human choice but, like all abilities and as Jesus taught in the parable of the talents, are meant to be used for the glory of our Master. When we offer any kind of "talent" to God from Whom it came, He will direct its use and development.

It is true, as Lowell intimates, that I have always felt something urging me on to a higher way of life, but do not we all feel this? In my own case this inner urge was leading me toward spiritual healing, which always should include being channels for Christ's love and peace wherever we meet any type of human need.

Tearing down walls is another soul-desire of mine. Surely, we all recognize that anything divisive, whether between nations, races, churches or individuals, must be melted in the fire of God's Love. As for me, a wall is always a challenge, and I have discovered that healing, peace-making and tearing down walls fit together like pieces of the same puzzle and are, in truth, part of the same hope, the same vision of the Kingdom to come.

Discouragement and feelings of inadequacy are also common experiences; yet, all of us sometimes sense a pulling toward "peaks of attainment." Every soul is aware in varying degree of the cosmic urge within. The awareness may be only very occasional and the faintest of glimmers but, as we concentrate and develop this most vital area of ourselves, that which has been dim and almost unrecognized begins to grow toward its ultimate maturity.

Another subject touched upon in the next message is the power of two working together. Ideally, I believe marriage should become two blended lives working as one to unite with and to further the divine Oneness of Creation. In our marriage we have been greatly blessed and benefited by Lowell's loving spirit-assistance and by our vivid understanding that we three are united as a permanent team of

love. All our difficulties and personal adjustments have
served to cement the bond between us as well as to enrich our individual lives by drawing us closer to the Source
and Strength of all overcoming.

Sebasco Estates, Maine
September 22, 1947

"Mom, dearest Mom:

*"I sense the hunger-cry in your soul for a personal
message. Sometimes you feel I am far away, but this is not
so. I am in all the love thoughts, the pure thoughts, you
ever have. I am part of the very star for which you are
aiming. I am part of the urge within you to live more
freely and unselfishly. You can never lose me (yes, the
same 'me' who lived with you on earth). You believe I am
spirit. So I am, but spirit is warm and understanding, bearing within itself all the human personality traits which you
think I have outgrown. Are you not spirit, too, you and
Dad and every other person who lives to love and know
the Great Light? The same life was in you as a tiny baby,
a happy child, an adolescent and then a mature woman.
All are natural stages, wherein the spirit learns to manifest
itself through the rise and decline of the physical existence.
In the next stage, that of the released-land, we go right on
growing more like our own perpetual spirit-self, which constantly draws nearer to its ultimate transcendency.*

*"You think too much, you allow too many thoughts to
come into your mind. That is why you get confused and
feel, sometimes, your efforts are not worthwhile. Just accept
life, do not try to figure everything out. No human can
understand the whys and wherefores of everyday living.
Minds are delicate instruments to pick up the vibrations
which are the communication system of the invisible world.*

*Some minds are strongly built and able to withstand con-
tinued and rough use. Others are more sensitive and easily
shaken out of balance. All types have their use. To work
out world problems, all kinds of receiving sets are necessary.*

"Be thankful for your sensitivity, Mom, and do not ever
wonder how you can become less sensitive. You are attuned
to super-waves of inspiration; your work is to absorb them
and give them to others. This you cannot do when you
allow an entrance to the inharmonious, lower vibrations of
the world. You must learn to cut these off. You have been
given instructions about this. You have, for your own use,
every facility of inspired consciousness to help you succeed.
Be more grateful for the cosmic power which is over, above
and within you.*

"Remember, you have attached yourself to ideals leading to a distant peak of illumination and attainment. If
you had not the inherent possibilities of reaching it, you
would not have that sublime urge to follow, step by step,
the difficult climb. If the climb seems steep, if the summit
ahead seems hidden in fogs, do not be discouraged and
say that it is too much for you. Rest on your climb, wait
for the fogs to clear, look back and realize how much
is behind you, and say a joyful prayer of gratitude. Rest
and gratitude bring new strength and new hope. You can
never go back, for home is here awaiting your return. Your
heart-longings to be nobler are but the calling homeward to
Itself of the Mother-Father-God. When you stay on your
own path and follow your sure intuition, your way is lighted
and clear. It is only when you cast side glances at others'
paths that you temporarily wander off. Following another
human's path rather than your own brings only confusion.*

"You and Dad are blessed in that you have been relieved
of many material handicaps and that together you may*

express in words, action and writing those truths which are entrusted to you. Two lives, blended in desire to serve God's purposes first, are more potent than humans can know. Keep on with this as your supreme desire; do not look for human understanding or appreciation. The inner joy of such a relationship is reward in itself. Love gives itself for the joy of giving. Two dedicated lives may radiate light from the pure, spontaneous joy of being on fire with the Divine Spark. Where the light falls does not matter; that you both cherish the Light is enough.

"You want a personal word, Mom. To tell you that I am as near you as I ever was is unnecessary. You know, and knowing, you should sparkle inside with the realization that there is no time, distance nor space between us, now or ever. I have never 'passed over.' There is no 'over.' There is only an expansion, a drawing nearer to Reality. Here, in the less obstructed, less limited strata of consciousness, we follow the explorative urge which is the magnetic force of All-life drawing its own back to Itself.

"To bring less sensitive souls into this realization is your earth task. Therefore, let gratitude sing in your heart today that part of you, which is me, is where it belongs. Were I still on earth, we would be caught in temporary tangles of a more complicated life. With my being here to minimize your physical handicaps with assurance of their lack of importance, we can function together better than in an earth relationship. I am a link to higher influences. Were I not continually urging you to live above doubts, fears and human entanglements, I would be failing those whose love and guidance I am relaying. I have much to do, even as have you and Dad. You would not want to retard this mission by allowing any date to remind us of former grief. Rather, shall we not make this day a symbol of closer co-

*operation? Will you not draw nearer to me and to reality
today? Peace and happiness, which the world cannot know,
are here waiting for your receptivity. Their inflow will dissolve the daily irritations and perplexities which would bind
you to themselves. Cut yourself free from them; let us go
adventuring, as we planned to do in the earth days. It will
not be in an old Ford this time, Mom, nor in an airplane,
but it will be much more fascinating—we will go into the
lives and thoughts of higher souls who are working in direct
contact with the hallowed brothers of humanity who have
looked into the face of Christ and knelt in adoration before
His Omnipotence."*

38

BY THE FIRESIDE

On our way back to Coronado that year we stopped in Washington to visit my sister, May. May was living in Mother's old home and was keeping alive the same hospitable and loving atmosphere with which Mother had filled it. We all could still feel Mother's influence and vital personality about the house as a lingering blessing. On this particular night, May and I were sitting by the fire, as Mother had loved to do. It seemed only natural that she should join us there and speak words of motherly affection into our thoughts.

Washington, D. C.
October 29, 1947

"My two sweet daughters:

"Yes, I am gathered unto you, hovering by the fireside, warm and outstretching like the fire glow, yet I am silent to human ears as are the shadows thrown by the fire itself. You felt me last night. You thought of me as a gray shadow, poignant and far away. Think no more of me that way, for I am flaming fire intensified. I burn with loving desire within hearts open to me and within hearts open to my understanding and my suggestions. I go forth timelessly into adventuring; I go forth to far peaks of illumination. Earth searching is but kindergarten compared to the boundless magnitude of opportunity here. Earth knows but the A B C's of existence, which are mere sips of the soul-

satiating drinks of wisdom, knowledge and love we find here. I would bring refreshing drinks to burning earth desires. Where better would I go adventuring than into the hearts of my own daughters?"

39

UNCLE BOB

The next message concerns our beloved friend, Bishop Harris, known as Bob or Uncle Bob to his numerous friends. Those who knew Bob will never forget him. His searching and compassionate eyes seemed to see and understand deeply, and his delightful sense of humor never failed to enchant. He was a man filled with God but also a down-to-earth man filled with lovable human traits and habits. Very quiet about himself, his knowledge and his experiences, Bob had a wonderful way of drawing the best out of others and of making people feel that they had something to offer. He had great ability in making others know the vital nearness of our Creator, and the divine touch was revealed most of all in the simplicity and the naturalness of anything he said or did.

One of Bob's very human joys in life was duck hunting, and he and Franklin were often shooting companions. About two weeks before the next message came to me, we were approaching Coronado after our cross-country trip from Maine. Franklin was looking forward with his usual enthusiasm to an already planned hunting excursion with Bob, and we were both anticipating Thanksgiving which we were to spend with him and his wife, Mary, at their ranch. Despite our natural desire that day to reach home after our long journey, we decided to go to see them first because I was being constantly urged from within to do so. Bob happened to be at home alone, and we had a joyful reunion and a most satisfying talk. As we regretfully arose to leave, our hearts were very grateful for our warm welcome home and for our intimate association with this man. Bob came to the door with us and we noticed, and later remarked upon, an unusual depth of tenderness and near wistfulness in his affectionate farewell.

The next day Bob suffered a severe stroke and never spoke again. The following message from the spirit world was written during the first weeks of his long illness.

Coronado, California
November 29, 1947

"Child one of pondering, we are ever present to help bridge the gap between the articulate and the inarticulate, the seen and the unseen, the temporary and the eternal. The servant of God, whom so many love, hovers between the two phases of life. He is being prepared for reality beyond earth's painful limitations. His cycle of earth span has run its completed course. The light is fading from the temple of his body; it is being drawn, by magnetic force, back to the greater intensity of the pure light and love of God. The old garment, or earth body, has served its usefulness and is being discarded in preparation for a new, more radiant vehicle of expression. All is ready here; hosts of updrawing brothers of light are rejoicing as the soul of one of God's beloved comes forth to its rightful place of victory and intensified energy.

"This withdrawing of the spirit from the body is a painful experience to you of earth-limited understanding. All growth is separation; all separation is painful because it is natural to cling to the familiar phases of life. The whole purpose of creation is growth, and growth is change. Those souls who fail to comprehend this law and who cling to the

familiar, temporary phases of existence are limiting the evolution of the races of men. The bodily vehicle goes through many complete changes in a lifetime. It is through these changes that the spirit expands, absorbs truth and is prepared for the final separation of spirit from body. Think of the many handicapped ones who never lose their infantile conception of life. Resenting the changes of development, they cling to immaturity and are prisoners of their own dormant consciousness, thus becoming deterrants to God's great plan of evolution. They are the fearful, who look to the light held by earth hands rather than to the inner light which is nurtured and controlled by the great cosmic light. They resent and fear change, especially death, which is the abrupt and final severing of the familiar.

"Not so those who follow the march of God's great purposes and who search to reveal His purposes in their own lives. Blessed are you who are near this soul, now in the valley; blessed are you who have released him with joyful trust. Your faith and love are providing wings for his spirit, facilitating his flight to the higher strata of consciousness. The living faith of his Mary is a burning flame, cleansing earth suffering and leaping in its purity to the fringes of eternity; she is dying to familiar, cherished earth happiness just as her husband is doing. She journeys with him the dark road, which to unawakened mortals seems the end of hopes and dreams. We bid her wait patiently until the return current of God's peace and joy enters her heart."

40

BALANCE

The next three messages deal with balance. The first is from Lowell, and the other two are from unknown spirit-friends. All three suggest, in differing phraseology, that true balance is a facet of perfection and therefore of the most delicate make-up and fluidity.

Coronado, California
December 20, 1947

"Mom, I come to help you disentangle yourself from earth pressure. When I was a baby toddling about, I often sprawled flat on earth because my balance was immature. You picked me up with loving hands and kissed away my baby grief, just as you did in the dream last night. Gradually that lack of balance grew to maturity, and I walked upright in swinging rhythm. Could I do less for you when through pressure of earth demands you momentarily lose your balance? The darkness of earth problems is drawing you in the way gravitation draws man to the earth. The desire to reach out and touch the heights of the ideals entrusted to you lifts you above the laws of material living. Only true soul and body balance can withstand this two-way pulling.

"When you ignore the rules of the body temple, energy is sapped and the pull of the psychic or spirit force, trying to compensate, throws the mind into confusion. I would lift you with loving understanding and give you wings of

light to help you know more clearly the laws of balance. Do not resent or abuse the laws of the physical body. It is the shrine where the spirit functions. It must be cherished, loved and regulated by laws of living which cannot be overleapt any more than man can disregard the laws of gravitation. Restore your bodily temple with rest, relaxation, fresh air and joy-filled exercise. When it is fully restored, demands made on you will not weaken and confuse you. You will, instead, have a natural, happy outflowing of released energy. This balance will bring peace, power, keenness of direction, clear thinking and joyful activity.

"The law of the whole universe is Balance. The suns and planets swing in celestial balance, attuned to God's laws of momentum. What would happen if the laws fell out of balance?—disintegration. What happens to a human being when the laws of earth existence are thrown out of balance with the spiritual laws? Confusion sets in, followed by disintegration of the Divine purpose struggling to grow and flourish in every human soul.

"As long as you are of the world, your feet must tread earth ways; your roots must be firm in its soil, even though your soul growth bids you reach toward the sun. Earth soil is rich in nourishment of lessons to be learned. Absorb quickly earth's necessary contributions so that from them will grow the strong stem and the blossom of beauty. This will be the soul bursting into maturity. When man leaves earth life, he carries with him that which he has plucked from earth growth. The balance between the two, the absorbing of earth nourishment (earth lessons learned) and the soul-stretching toward the light, is the combination which brings into fulfillment the perfection of the blossom."

Coronado, California
December 22, 1947

*"You must keep a perfect balance between the material,
demanding world and the invisible world of light and spirit.
Never forget your obligations to the physical and outward
expression of transitional life. As you live in the physical
world of the senses, let it reflect the eternal, spiritual universe. As you think, dream and focus your consciousness, so
shall reality come. From creation to present flow of re-
creation, inner consciousness always produces concrete
forms; never do concrete forms produce consciousness.
Your thoughts are the wires through which the Creator
flashes His creative light, and your mind is the receiving set
of this cosmic force.*

*"As you live gladly, warmly and actively, let your heart
glow with the realization that it is illuminated by the creative flow of Divine consciousness. Love both the creative
force and its visible creations. Look for beauty in love and
truth as you look for beauty in nature. Beauty is food for
the unseen man, the spirit of man. It is just as essential as
food for the physical. When man goes rooting about in
darkness, giving power to evil designs and criticizing or
judging his fellow man, he is furthering the starvation of
his own soul. On the other hand, praise and gratitude are
the garnishers of spiritual nourishment and help bring about
God's perfect balance."*

Coronado, California
January 19, 1948

*"Faith in God is a flower which must be nurtured before
its tiny shoots can reach out and cling to the hard wall of
life. Christ said, 'Faith without works is dead.' He did not*

mean that activity alone is the force which increases faith. He did mean that working, longing and asking are the means of stimulating and increasing faith until it accomplishes the seemingly impossible. The 'works' referred to are not only bustling human activities but the rushing of the soul toward faith to accomplish its invisible activity. Remember always that it is faith which releases healing answers to situations, problems and health. Human expressions of kindness and love are merely the levers to lift the law of fulfillment above earth shadows. It is faith itself which gives wings for release from dark shadows.

"Faith knows no defeats. Faith does not look to human wisdom for its healing force. Faith looks straight to God, to whom nothing is impossible. According to your faith is a miracle born instantaneously or slowly. Examine your own faith daily. Do you ask, in the name of Christ, for the perfect solution and then relax and know that invisible forces of good are beginning their work of healing and that they will show you your part; or do you ask and then take too much personal responsibility by rushing unguidedly into action? Answer this for yourself, but let it sink into your conscious and subconscious mind that power comes from being still and knowing rather than from human activity.

"Faith is nurtured in silence. Works of faith are the expanding natural fulfillment of the universal law of love. Since love fashions all, knows all, is all, how can humans doubt that the law of love expresses itself through them? Doubts arise when you focus your desire-love on the objective rather than on the power of love itself. The God of Love is inexhaustible; man in pouring forth energy becomes exhausted unless he is receiving in perfect balance the inflow of spirit from the source of all love. It is through the channel of faith that love is regulated. If your efforts are *not bringing about harmonious solutions to your own and others' problems, you may be sure that there is not balance between your human works and the inflow of God's operative law of love.*

"Since faith is a flower evolving toward perfection, love guides the creative force. Man can do no more than plant the seed of faith and nurture it; God's creative power is the means of its growth and flourishing."

41

HACIENDA DE LUZ

The Harris ranch house was called "Hacienda de Luz" and could not have been more appropriately named. It was a house of light even during its construction, for it was built entirely by men seeking help for all types of problems. Although Mary and Bob had influenced many lives, at this period God seemed to send to them men who were endowed with practical abilities as to house building. Through sharing in the construction of the ranch, men out of work, men with differing personal problems, were helped. As lives were changed and problems healed, carpentry or plumbing or whatever skills were needed were opportunely provided. The Harris' contagious faith took deep root, and joy and laughter often furnished necessary release from emotional tensions. Quiet talk, prayer, patience, love and understanding were in abundance.

Franklin and I increasingly realize how much we absorbed and learned at the ranch. It was built on top of a mountain overlooking quiet valleys and the hills of Mexico; wild lilacs were our especial delight, and in memory we can still vividly see Bob's yellow roses. The grandeur of nature suggested to us vistas beyond human knowledge just as the peace and joy of the ranch itself were beyond ordinary understanding. Here we learned more of real Christian fellowship and outgoingness. Mary's love-filled hospitality will never be forgotten, nor will our many quiet hours of prayer.

We still picture Bob sitting on his porch surrounded by his climbing roses. Smoking his pipe and gazing out over the nearby mountains, his eyes are deep with far-away thoughts and dreams. Everything about him suggests the wisdom and peace of eternity, and none of us wants to interrupt his reverie. Often he tells us that peace is his dream. He envisions God's Kingdom spread over all the earth; he dreams of the reign of the Prince of Peace, of the Christ who said,

"Peace I give unto you; My peace I leave with you. Not as the world giveth, give I unto you; let not your heart be troubled, neither let it be afraid."

On February 7, 1948, after his long illness, Bob left us to go on to the next life. Regardless of our natural and acute yearning for his earthly companionship, we rejoiced that his spirit was now free to carry on in the larger existence. Six days later the following message was expressed through me.

Coronado, California
February 13, 1948

"Does it matter if truth comes in small streams or in rushing currents? It is the same truth. A mental attitude of calmness and a spiritual attitude of joy and gratitude stimulate the inflow of true inspiration. Let the time element go, the where-you-are-at-the-moment attitude; put into your conscious mind the idea which is already in your super-conscious mind. There is no separation in reality between carnate and discarnate souls; all rest now and forever in the resourcefulness of God Himself.

"Release Bob, that soul of lighted purposes, to universal love everytime you think of him. He is so surrounded by earth friends, many of whom love him without vision, that

he is not completely free as yet. He is not earth-bound, but earth-loved. His great capacity for inhaling and exhaling pure love has drawn so many earth children to him that it is difficult for him to disentangle himself from their magnetic longings. You who are releasing all earth ties with silent, intuitive impulses of joy are aiding him. You are also helping to lift him into the intensified flame of light where he is being revitalized. His is not a going-on to new glories but is, rather, a return to old familiar existence. He is busy making adjustment to dear ones here and to a higher sublimity of consciousness. The majority of his earth-friends do not understand and are dwelling on memories and earthly love. This acts as a magnetic pull back to his old life. He does not want to be pulled back, for he has been ready for a long time to go on to the new life for which he has been preparing himself. All of you who sense the higher laws of universal love must act as a unified force to dissolve lack of understanding in others.

"Many great men, whom the masses idolize, find it difficult to adjust to the plane where they find themselves upon awakening. The weight of masses of unilluminated souls, mourning and rebelling, pulls them back to earth. Westerners are far behind, are almost primitive, in their conception of death. Orientals have the gift of releasement within themselves, although they dress it up in fantastic garments. They have the unified faith of little children that their idols and dear ones are stepping into their conception of heaven, just as the American Indian had of the passing of souls into the 'happy hunting ground.' Such beliefs are better, incomplete and stilted as they are, than the lack of belief of worshippers of the human intellect. Westerners too often have faith only in material things and reject what

*cannot be proved. Orientals have a deep inherent faith and
are thus more susceptible to spiritual impulses.*

*"With all your combined faith, you must release Bob.
The phases of his earth life and of his passing through the
vale of suffering are over. He is now gloriously awakened
to old familiar realities. He is flooded by such intensity of
lighted love that earth ties seem like a dream. His vibrations
are so stepped up, his consciousness so blinded by revitaliza-
tion, that for a while he will rebel against earth pullings.
Mary feels the reflection of his joy, and her complete de-
tachment is the greatest proof of her love. He is surrounded
by the Saints of all-time, wrapped in their very beings. His
was such a welcome as to startle and confuse him momentarily. His guides will aid in the orientation of his soon-to-
be-chosen work. The silver thread of love which binds him
to Mary and you loved ones on earth is fragile, yet powerful. It will bind even more strongly as time goes on. Do not
pull on this cord of love; wait until Bob's readjusted consciousness is clarified and directed back into earth love.
When time is ripe, many will be transformed by his transforming love. It will have far greater power than when he
lived on earth.*

*"This is a time for rejoicing, not for grieving over per-
sonal and temporary ties. Sing a song of triumph. Many
will catch its strain and thus live closer to reality, losing
their limited vision of death. You who already know are
stewards of the greatest gift Christ brought, the gift of immortality. As you share this gift, time, space and death will
be forgotten and, in their place, will come the communion
of Saints and the deep-desire urge to join in their march
toward the light. The Saints ever bid you to pick up the
stragglers, the lost, the blind and to show them the silver
pathway of God's love. Bless every earth experience, how-*

ever bitter, which increases your capacity to receive the light of the Prince of Peace. His light is more luminous and more impelling when man sees Him in spite of darkness. Be grateful for having known so well this man who now is enfolded in Christ's light. Another soul is back home from its earth-journey, another star is shining in the sky. From that star's mystic ray shall glad tidings come to you on earth. Rejoice and sing songs of praise and thanksgiving."

42

THE UPWARD CLIMB

Often writings from Lowell have come through to me on special days. The next one was received on Mothers' Day just as we were about to leave for church. I was wearing my new spring hat, my gloves were in my hand, but I could not deny the strong impulse to type a message. In less than ten minutes this Mothers' Day greeting from my son came to me almost like a dictated letter. His affectionate understanding and his urging us on to a higher and purer love toward all life made my heart glow.

Coronado, California
May 9, 1948

"Dear Mom, greetings to this day on which minds dwell intensely on mother-love. In spite of commercialization of this vulnerable emotion, in spite of many who remember halfheartedly, in spite of any insincerity, this day is truly significant. It awakens deep-seated memories of the least-sullied love which God has released on earth, that of mother for child. Hearts are focused on unselfish love, and this transforming emotion radiates strength and healing.

"I have not forgotten, and never will forget, my relationship with my own earth Mother and Dad. I tingle with joy at happy memories. Those memories and that earthly love launched me into the ways of universal mysteries. I was nourished by earth experience and grew strong enough to weather the challenges of the higher life. Your love fitted

*me for greater opportunities and greater service here just
as kindergarten forms the foundation for higher schools of
learning on earth.*

*"During recent years our love has been translated into
many phases of your earth experience. It has lifted you and
Dad above valleys of despair and fogged-in areas of uncertainty. It has aided your climb up the steep mountain-
side and is still urging you on and on. It will never cease
being a driving force for you both. As my own capacity to
receive and absorb truth, love and light increases, the urge
to relay them back into earth life accelerates. Do not be
misled by evil's subtle propaganda which reacts as a seda-
tive to distract and dull minds that need to be alert. Peace
will not come until the good in men's hearts is nurtured
into maturity. There is no substitute for God's indwelling
love. Ethical, civic, scientific and even religious movements
are not alone sufficient to bring the peace which man so
desperately needs. Nothing will bring this peace except the
expansion of each human heart into a replica of God's love.*

*"Let it be your Mothers' Day resolve to enfold your
human love into the love of Christ. Your own efforts toward
a dedicated life may seem to you a small contribution toward great world problems, but it is your one responsibility.
Radiations from even one love-filled life reach beyond
human ken. So today, my once-Mom, I give myself, my
illumination, my yearning and my wisdom to you that the
impact may awaken you to my joy.*

*"Come often with the Master to the heights and dwell
on the vision of God; then will the breath of the higher
life serve to carry you through the denser levels of everyday experiences. Let your spirit feed on the pure air of the
heights even when you walk in the lowlands among the
suffering. Walk with compassion rather than with sym-*

*pathy. Compassion is detached sympathy which lifts suf-
fering ones to the love of God. Often suffering is a tool
which is instrumental in an individual's growth and healing. You must love every experience, even symptoms of
suffering; they may lead to fashioning a new and better
life-pattern. We are a composite of our successes and failures, which has evolved into a beautiful or ugly pattern
depending on the direction of our wills and on the precision
with which we have used our tools. Man can choose how
he will live. The human will is God's gift which bears man
away from or toward God's perfect will, his own highest
good.*

*"Many you wish to help have not oriented their wills to
the released will of God, they have not surrendered the
meanderings of self-will. Until they have, do not spend too
much energy on them. Love them and relinquish them,
blessing their temporary suffering as a cleansing fire which
sooner or later will purify their attitudes and desires. I beg
of you to free yourself from some of these unalerted earth
souls, who are a drain to your strength, and to give them
into divine control. This freeing, this relinquishment, will
help all concerned toward greater progress."*

43

DIVINE RESTRAINT

I include the next message from a helpful spirit because it enlarges upon some of the thoughts of the preceding chapter. We were trying during the summer to help a young man, through prayer and counseling, to find his true self and his God. In our enthusiasm one day we became too eager to convince our friend, thus confusing and upsetting him. The following writing came to me a few hours later as I struggled to discover the reasons for our blunder. It quieted my troubled mind and put added emphasis on the importance of both restraint and relinquishment.

Human enthusiasm, we learn, can be dangerous when self-opinion becomes the ruling factor. None of us intend to give self entrance into God's work, but enthusiasm sometimes carries us beyond the point of true sensitivity to His leading. The error becomes intensified if we influence a seeking soul to accept our own standards and desires. Be these ever so worthwhile, we have yet failed in our mission, for there is no substitute in any life for individual contact with one's own inner source.

Coronado, California
July 15, 1948

"You must learn to understand Divine restraint and to rely on this quality of love. Indifference is something else; it suggests coldness, aloofness and separation from love. Divine restraint, on the other hand, is the understanding,

compassionate patience of God's Love which waits for the perfect moment of attunement. Our Father never rushes in to answer until the door is opened, no matter how slightly, from within. Imbued with their own interpretation of God's spirit, humans often rush in when doors are not yet open to love and thus walk where 'angels fear to tread.'

"God never hurries, is never demanding or impatient; He never wavers from the supreme, eternal laws of fulfilling love. God never forces the flowers to bloom. He merely sends sunshine, rain and the needed elements of growth so that the law will fulfill itself. In spite of eagerness, enthusiasm and good intentions, you must learn not to rush in where there are closed doors. When a door gently swings open to the hand of love, then is the time to respond.

"Do not be discouraged or personally chastened; rather, thank God that through more sensitivity to the spirit's directing and through mistakes such as today's, He is teaching you His restraint. You must use this quality in dealing with urges to help people and with methods to unfold situations, also in dealing with any kind of suffering for, through suffering, God's purposes are often brought to fruition. Divine restraint contains no self-feelings to cause confusion and frustration. Relinquishment of self-desires leads to God's will, which includes His timing as well as His healing and His glorification.

"Learn quickly, for there is much to do. Time is ever calling closer and closer those who love Christ. Rejoice, be exceedingly grateful that your lessons are becoming harder and more exacting; they are the result of efforts to obey and overcome. Sing with gratitude and ignore all thoughts and actions save those of the spirit of love which runs like a golden river through all that is."

44

JOY, THE MOTHER OF LIFE

During all the years of the world's suffering from war
and its aftermath, the years so full of frustration, fear and
heartbreak, my messages from the next world continued to
dwell upon the importance of the spirit of joy. We are
urged to drink of the eternal well-springs of joy even in
the darkest days, for "The Light still shines in the darkness,
and the darkness has never put it out."

Coronado, California
August 23, 1948

*"We are waiting for a clearer atmosphere in your con-
sciousness before we can continue our lessons of Light. Do
not feel guilty about this delay, for time is strengthening
your desire to continue on the road of illumination. All is
preparation; patience is as necessary as talent, willingness
and perseverance. They all belong together. Learn from
every circumstance wherein you find yourself, then will
those circumstances open the door to fulfillment of life's
purposes.*

*"Frustration has opened more doors to victory than any
other secular or spiritual experience. Frustration makes man
willing to accept, according to his capacity, that for which
his soul yearns. He thus embraces discipline as well as opportunity to grow.*

*"Be on guard against scattering your efforts. Temptations
will come in many guises. You are to concentrate on clear-*

ing your mind and uncluttering it from material debris so that you can catch the creative rhythm of joy which silently and insistently bids you to tarry on the mountain top. Do not be afraid to accept this joy which calls you. It is the mother of life and the womb from which you sprang. It is an outcalling echo bidding you to return to your own destiny. The world is dark because it has forgotten from whence it came and whither it goes. Created in joy, the world responds on a wave length of joy and suffers when child-like simplicity and joy are lost.

"For the many oppressing problems of the world today, joy provides an answer as simple as the laughter of a child. Your Creator, your Father-Friend, your Mother-Protector, made you for joy, not for adversity and inharmony. Blessed is he who is innately aware of this truth, for he can then look beyond the brooding offspring of mental pondering to the eternal purposes of life. Joy comes from within, not in response to earth conditions or accomplishments; joy comes from the realization of the oneness of all life and from the mingling of currents of energy and love. God is perfection and, as His child, you are free to inhale and exhale the very essence of His Mind."

45

INNER SEEING

Less than a month later, we were in church when the following message came from Bob Harris. For me, writing on church calendars has been a fairly common experience, for I cannot resist any insistent appeal of truth which seeks expression through me. On this particular Sunday I well remember seeing Bob and Lowell together for the first time. The music and the inspiration of the service lifted me into another dimension where my inner eye could recognize their two figures in a luminous light. As with most "visions" seen with invisible eyes, I was aware of a joyous pulsation; my higher self seemed to merge with that radiance which partially veiled the larger-than-life bodies of those two dearly loved ones.

Christ Church
Coronado, California
September 19, 1948

"Can you not see us at the altar? Deep concentration of loving forces can lift you to our plane. Yes, you see in the dazzling light Lowell's boyish spirit resurrected into its true stature. He asked me to come here with him. Lowell has been trying to increase your awareness in many ways. He and I, together with a host of choir angels, are blended in the love at the altar with such intensity that you feel it. You see us—not with the physical eye, but with the spirit eye.

"All is well. Great light is pouring into earth darkness.

Earth is living out all that has been already won and lived on the higher planes of existence. God's purposes can never fail. He is, always has been, always will be, in control, but man's blindness obscures this truth. Whereas you on earth can see but dimly 'as through a glass darkly,' our Creator's purposes are being fulfilled now. Have no fear, relax amid the darkness. Relax and become more awakened. The perfect answer must come from the invisible world; you will need spiritualized sight to see, spirit's wisdom to know and understanding love to awaken the sleeping ones.

"We are very near you; we permeate your earth plane. Do not isolate us as unreal and strange. We are not different now, merely transcended into reality. Lowell and I come together many times, and we often recall earth experiences. Lowell is free to see beyond your self-bondage and to express your true heart-longings. He is a part of your heart-longing. All servants of truth who answer the call of God's love are echoing the real, unvoiced thoughts of creation.

"Love all life, love all types of souls, love all the stragglers on the path of awakenment. Work for and dream of unity—unity in purpose, in ideals, in dedication. Let unimportant personality traits vanish like mist. Look for the seed personality, the God-self, within each person and unite with it. All barriers must go. All who love God must unite, for the day of salvation, of true world peace, is near at hand. Rejoice and know."

46

FRINGES OF CONSCIOUSNESS

When I read *The Man From Lebanon* by Barbara Young, I found learning about Kahlil Gibran a thrilling experience. His life, his mystical awareness, the beauty of his soul-expression struck in me chords deeper than memory and lifted me out of my everyday self. That night a dream-adventure in which I seemed to reach new areas of perception came to me with a reality of sharper focus than the wakeful actualities of this world. The next morning my tumbling thoughts produced the following sentences, which seem to fit naturally with those of the preceding message from Bob Harris.

Coronado, California
January 15, 1949

"Your experience last night was no dream. It was I, Gibran, who touched ever so lightly the fringes of your consciousness. From there I called upon the higher vibrations of thought and upon the effervescent currents of life. What you thought were dreams was your own consciousness soaring into new flights. Once an earth soul tastes this ethereal substance, this light force, it never rests until it tastes it again.

"What you experienced was the soul's flight into the fourth dimension. A human being knows depth, height and thickness, but a spirit sublimates these dimensions and lifts the earth-pulled vibrations up into the eternal dimension.

"The most powerful energy in the universe is the mind of God. No human could contact it without disintegration of his physical senses. However, when this energy is deflected on a lower ray and at a lower rate of speed, it can penetrate minds still in the physical-body state. All the rays of Divine consciousness are centered in Christ. The force of His Being can flow to meet a desire-call from any mind in the universe. Christ-energy metes out that fraction or that infinitesimal portion of energized thought which is appropriate for the instrument into which it flows. The instrument, man, must be attuned and ready for the inflow. 'Ask and ye shall receive' means that from the reservoir of spirit man receives no more than he is capable of accepting.

"Therefore, the more continually man asks and makes himself fit to receive, the more he lives in the world of spirit, the world of the fourth dimension. In this dimension, physical laws are not set aside but are super-directed. The natural laws of the material world are sublimated in spiritual laws. The results are not miracles but merely the laws of the fourth dimension overruling the laws of physical life. The laws of the fourth dimension created man, sustain him and release him at so-called death. These laws cannot be learned from books or by word of mouth. They come as an inner unfolding to the man who searches for Divine Truth."

47

THE ARMY OF LIGHT

When the next message was written, our new, smaller house was nearing completion. The time had seemed right to give up our larger home because of its strenuous upkeep, and we had been able to do so without undue regret. Again our house was built under prayer; again the workmen responded, and satisfactory progress was the result. Before we moved in May, we had prayers of dedication, and thus began a new chapter for the three of us.

Coronado, California
April 1950

"Mom, we need your help here, so please put all your spiritual strength into action. We are lining up in the invisible world, as you are on the earth planet, to fight the greatest penetration of darkness ever known. Be alerted, all you souls who long to flood the earth with light that it may survive the disintegrating powers of darkness.

"We here are constantly sending light into individuals, and each soul infused with this spiritual force becomes one of the great Army of Light. These souls are being prepared for the coming titanic struggle, just as soldiers are equipped for battle. In this bloodless war, nerves and hearts are being steeled with divine armor. We are striving endlessly to prevent the shedding of blood in another human war, and we need each soul capable of using all his faith as a solvent for the world's greed and hate.

"Footsteps into eternity always lead toward the Light. Those who are under evil domination and who walk away from the Light must be viewed with compassion rather than with condemnation. Hate the evil designs in their misguided consciousness, but love their souls. Help them by your own steadfastness to turn away from the insecurity of darkness to the All-Light. Try to free them from the bindings of hate, lust, greed and other fruits of darkness. Each soul redeemed speeds the day of the world's re-creation into God's pattern. Your way to help dissolve hate, selfishness and indifference is to be a joyous channel of love and warmth.

"These qualities are evident in your new home, which is blessed and which reflects the love and beauty you have put into it. You need not be overly concerned about its furnishings and upkeep, but you should revel in the joy of its open arms. I know it will be a magnet to draw those who need the blessings which God has given you. Can you not feel me helping to draw them?

"I love you and all the earth, but I love the world of spirit more. Please relay my messages and send forth gladness. I am the song in your heart, and we are together in eternity. Eternity is not some distant time nor place but is now—forever is now."

48

RESURRECTION

Newness of life, ecstatic renewal of joy, Easter once again. Our Risen Lord in Resurrection Glory permeates our beings with His Own glad Heart. His love sings within as we realize anew that He has vanquished death and given us Eternity. Easter, 1950, is a day of remembered joy, a day of happy hearts, a day in which Lowell describes our Master's triumph in the following words.

Coronado, California
Easter, 1950

"God never limits the power of his disciples; they limit themselves by their withdrawal from Him. They also limit those they would help by dwelling on the very conditions which are imprisoning them. Easter, the day of Resurrection, stands as a symbol of release for all men and should be a perpetual challenge.

"Easter time should not primarily be regarded as a time for reviewing the events of Christ's earthly life but should be looked upon, with praise and wonder, as a time of metamorphosis and renewal. The world itself and all life within it is in a continual state of resurrection. Age-old patterns like prejudice, selfishness and despair are put to sleep by man's refusal to harbor them. From this sleep comes rebirth. The world is continually being reborn amidst its pain and darkness. How else could earth consciousness be lifted to release new visions?

"There is joy in death, in the death of such evils as sickness, hatred, jealousy and bigotry. All evil shall die, and a new heaven and earth shall emerge. Know this, feel it, demonstrate it in your own lives; then, your contagious spirit will infect others with new hope.

"Easter is triumph; overcoming is triumph. Death is triumph because He, our Risen Lord, has made it so."

49

SPIRITUAL HEALING

During the next three or four years, I was concentrating on healing work and on writing. Although the following is one of the few personal messages from Lowell in this period, I know he was often instrumental in helping me to receive impersonal, more universal thoughts.

I am interested in reconsidering the words below which Lowell relays from Bob Harris to our "little group." By this time we were closely associated with many whose lives were dedicated to the ministry of healing. Believing healing to be a definite part of Christ's mission, His commandment to preach the gospel and heal the sick was our inspiration. Sick in body, mind or spirit covers the gamut of human suffering. In healing work our way is to offer ourselves as channels for God's love. We are often led to give of ourselves to those prayed for in practical loving-kindness, but always prayer and sensitivity to God's leading are the essentials. Complete relinquishment to God is another vital factor in successful healing work. God alone is the healer, and we can be used by Him effectively only as we get ourselves and our own ideas out of the way so that He can work through us. All love is healing, and surely our churches follow but half of Christ's injunction when they preach the gospel of love but fail to use His power to heal. We, in this movement, long to see healing back in the churches as it was in the earliest Christian era.

At about this time, Franklin and I attended a "Camp

Farthest Out", a healing camp at Forest Home in California. Under the leadership of Glenn Clark, medical doctors, psychiatrists, nurses, ministers and lay people participated. Lectures and training for healing work were followed by a clinic for patients. This furnished thrilling examples of Christ's healing power and, at Forest Home, both of us received stimulation in our faith and belief. Here our sense of purpose became more fully established concerning spiritual healing. Intervening years have but strengthened our desire to be used as channels for His healing love.

We have been greatly privileged to know and work with some of the leaders in spiritual healing. I have mentioned John Gayner and Ethel Banks before. He was the Founder and first Warden of the "Order of St. Luke the Physician," of which we are members. The Order is an international, interdenominational organization dedicated to all phases of Christian Healing and to restoring it to its rightful place in the church. The present Warden is Dr. Alfred W. Price, rector of St. Stephen's Episcopal Church of Philadelphia. Under his inspired leadership Christian healing within the church has grown tremendously. Dr. Price's dynamic vision and personality have also awakened much interest and cooperation in this field within medical and professional circles.

In the next message I feel sure that the "test of service" predicted refers to the loss on this plane of John Gayner Banks and several other of our leaders within the ensuing few years. Among these are Glenn Clark, Rebecca and Wally Beard, Albert Cliffe and Rufus Moseley. The truth is that these leaders in their present existence are using their increased power to assist those on earth who are continuing the work they pioneered. Their co-operation and guidance have definitely been known, and interest in spiritual healing has grown far beyond our most hopeful early dreams.

Coronado, California
September 22, 1950

"Dearest Mom, you went to sleep praying for me and my closer relationship with our God. Bless you. Yes, this is Lowell speaking, but a Lowell so at one with many greater souls that I have become a tiny part of the Spirit of Truth. I know the ups and downs of your consciousness. I know the deep, hidden-from-the-world loneliness you and Dad have to overcome at times. Your efforts to replace loneliness with service strengthen the bond between us.

"You wonder what I am doing now. There is nothing mystical or strange about my now-existence; in fact, it is no stranger than yours. My spirit is constantly expanding and looking ahead to greater opportunities. Neither on earth nor on any of the many planes through which each soul must travel can we fully understand God's purposes or His yearning for His children. To fathom God's purposes would be to become God. We are all progressing, but we never will arrive until we are completely transformed into God's perfection. When that will be, none of us knows. Nevertheless, we are on our way, bound together by a silver cord of truth and light. We are one, evolving toward the element from which we are created.

"You must not be ashamed or apologetic for your failures and feelings of inadequacy. This is a common experience for all seekers. Man can never see his own growth; furthermore, he can not expand if he is stretching with pride at his own accomplishments. He must be willing to be unimportant and ineffectual according to world stand-

ards, for God's power comes through as individual unfoldment becomes a keener tool for the good of all.

"You are truly alive only when you are conscious of the
oneness of all life. When you pour yourselves into the life
of your brothers, you learn your absolute dependence on
the source of all life for replacement of that outpouring.
You should never feel tired when you are expending your
energy as God directs. But no matter how kind and loving
the motive or how fine the deed, you can become exhausted
if you are not obeying your inner voice. How can you become more expert in listening to and obeying this voice,
you are asking. Only by going into the absolute silence of
the inner chamber of your own self and tarrying there until
truth comes with assurance. Wait on the Lord; wait even
if you are in a crowd or in the midst of confusion and
hurry, wait on Him. You will be rewarded. 'They that wait
on the Lord shall renew their strength; they shall mount up
with wings as eagles. They shall run and not be weary;
they shall walk and not faint.' A special time and place to
concentrate is not always required. Rather, develop the
habit of expecting an inner voice to speak at any time or
place. Mom, you and I have always loved adventure, and
listening to God is life's greatest adventure. You have no
idea what lies ahead, or else you would sing for joy every
moment of your life.

"Uncle Bob, who is one of your guardian angels, says
that no memories are lost, for they are preserved in the
great book of life, someday to be reread as well as re-
experienced. He bids me send his love and say that your
little group on earth is being prepared for a real test of
service. Do not fear any tests, he says, but bless them all,
embracing them with your faith and love.

"The world is in a vacuum of emotion; hate and love are

in a death struggle. You must not mingle your emotions too often with the suffering, but you must continue to lift all suffering, confusion and darkness up to the Light. Others may have a seemingly more practical way of helping, but this is your way. Your healing touch will be accentuated as you use it, your energy will expand as it goes forth into channels of usefulness, your faith will grow as you confidently expect greater results and your love will deepen as you expend it.

"'Lo, I am with you alway, even to the end of the world.' These are our Master's shining words for this dark time. Because He is, in truth, with us always, then all who dwell in His Presence will likewise be with us until the end of time. Lift all which is darkness up into the stream of Light. There will peace be found. There is the Kingdom of God, now being revealed to those who seek it.

"The Holy Comforter is that life which touches Christ-consciousness and is one with it. He has pure truth and often gives us individualized perception. On every side, when eyes are open, are proofs of God's enduring love and His desire to raise human love to His standards. He uses all means for this divine purpose, and none of them should surprise you. All souls who offer themselves are used. We on this plane know better than you on earth the healing power of unselfish love. It unleashes such dynamic power for good that nothing can withstand it. Therefore, love everyone, even the weak, the bitter and those filled with hatred and evil. Pray for the perfect reversal of love in their lives, its reversal toward good away from evil. You can help reverse the power in any child of darkness by continually, and with true faith, giving him love and understanding.

"Time on earth is short, but love is endless. Choose those things which are eternal, and do not be troubled by tem-

porary frustrations. All which is darkness now will become illuminated. Whether it be soon or after agonies of more wars depends on those who have seen the inner vision and are working and praying for its unfoldment."

50

THE PRICELESS JEWEL

The next message is one which came to me after a time of prayer and quiet with Franklin and Mary Harris. Dwelling in each human heart, our Lord speaks at such times with infinite tenderness to each one. In addition to intimate personal words, individual answers to a group desire are often amazingly similar and clear. On this day the longing to become more effective channels for God's wholeness had brought us together "in one accord."

Coronado, California
June 16, 1951

"The energy which is generated in a harmonious, loving prayer group such as this may be stored and drawn upon in need or emergency. The diffusion of rays which combine when there is sincerity of desire, harmony of thought and surrender to God's Will actually becomes a crystalized, invisible jewel. Just as the essence of white contains all tints of the rainbow, so this jewel-essence of spiritual attributes merges into a unit of energy, which travels forth as a powerful ray.

"You may hold this energy in your consciousness and call upon it at any time. See it as a filament of light going forth on the invisible wires of your desire into any darkness where its healing power is needed. This is wholeness coming from God's love and power in answer to your love and desire outreaching to Him.

"The more often two or three come together in outgoing love and prayer, the larger grows the reservoir of the power of Light within. Cherish this glow, this light within your beings, as the priceless jewel of life, for from it come healing and joy to nurture the sick world."

51

A PICTURE COMES TO LIFE

The morning of a day when Mary Harris was coming for an overnight visit, I stopped to look at a photograph of her husband who had now been in the next world for four years. An enlargement of a very life-like picture of Bob in his bishop's robes, the eloquent eyes impress even those who never knew him. To an intimate friend their impact is almost electric. With a rush of gratitude, my heart warmed as I thought of Bob and other dedicated ones who are such clear channels for the Christ-within. I thought of how whenever Mary, Franklin and I were together we shared a joyous sense of well-being. The hours of fellowship always held deep meaning and spiritual fulfillment. Certainly we were aware at these times of the blessing of Bob's vibrant personality and of his increased power to lift us and those in our hearts.

Suddenly I felt my spirit soaring into another dimension, and with my earthly eyes I could almost see Bob move and step out of the picture frame. Many times I have had a similar experience or sensation when looking into Lowell's eyes in one of his pictures. Obviously, spirit-awareness, when powerful enough, reacts upon the physical senses.

Coronado, California
April 8, 1952

"When you look at my picture, or Lowell's, and feel as if we are stepping out to speak to you, the picture itself

does not produce this effect. The love in your heart and memories of earthly associations lift you to the higher vibrations of the invisible world. Your personality vibration becomes intensified until it flows into ours, which is always with you. That is what happened a few minutes ago.

"As for your experience last night, that was also a withdrawal from the material world around you. You expanded your consciousness into the real invisible world which supersedes time and space. Here there is no separation of life; those you call 'dead' are as active as the living.

"The more intense and sincere your desire to live beyond human sense-perception, the more real becomes your cosmic interpretation of life. Last night your soul photographed marching figures forever linked by their common destiny, moving toward the magnetic light. Living and 'dead' often touch hands, progressing together in purpose, unity and love. When earth relationships seem to fail or are not adequate, know that there are hosts of lighted ones ready to lead the bewildered back to the pathway. Power comes when minds are fused. Minds fused in evil purposes or self-assertion are powerful instruments for evil fruits. Minds fused in love and harmony are a force for peace and integration.

"Wilda, heed this calling; all of you, prepare for coming events. Earth cannot continue as it is. The light of the souls dedicated to Christ is still too dim. We are trying to focus our ethereal beam upon you, but the fogs caused by apathy, hate, discord and self-seeking break the contact. However, we will get through, for we are stronger than ever here. Each of you who looks up into the expanded consciousness will receive God-power. You will become magnetized so that you may unite with the souls who serve on this higher plane.

"The light is so dazzling that you could not stand it now. Prepare your spiritual eyes by concentrating on the light you can behold at this stage of development. Often I am with you; Lowell is part of me and I part of him, but you are not always aware of our integrated pure essence of love which is pouring into you.

"You and Mary, bless you, have learned to linger with the invisible angels long enough for us to get through to help you. I am glad Mary is coming to see you, for you three are not together enough. Great power is generated when you pool your love and faith. We here need consecrated, harmonious prayer cells through which to release soothing, healing vibrations into a tightened world. The sun with all its force and power does not suddenly break into the darkness of night; rather, it comes gradually and rhythmically. In similar manner, spiritual light comes to those who wait and know, to those whose eyes are opened to see it. Great revelations are now ripe for unfoldment. Your greatest task is to receive and relay the truth coming through us from the Lord of heaven and earth. Man leads an inconsistent life; everything needed for comfort, harmony and beauty is provided, yet he often refuses to accept it. Those who are attuned to Christ's love must offer themselves as harmonizers to the multitudes who are off key. You know by now that His disciples must follow in His path of suffering. But, with His hand on theirs, the path does not seem hard; strength, even as from the manna sent to the children of Israel, will come to those who choose to follow Him at any cost.

"Men of love must serve as empty moulds into which the molten fire of Christ's purposes may be poured. A man-sized mould, full of human plans and answers, is not able to hold the true projections of God-mind. Therefore, you

*three must be emptied of everything but love so that we of
the Brotherhood of Christ may fill you until you overflow
with healing joy.*

*"You should not be overly concerned about your fluctua-
tions of health. The reason you and Franklin have setbacks
is that you are being pulled by two worlds. 'Pay it no
mind,' as our Mary says. 'Pay no mind' to limitations or
physical symptoms and do not wonder too much about
them. If understanding of the laws of healing came too
easily, you would not be as eager to grow and search.
When one stops growing and searching, he is more dead
than the lifeless sod. When one seeks God day and night,
then weakness becomes strength, then is one literally 'praying without ceasing.' Physical setbacks act as a thorn in the
heart to spur one on to new life and energy. In Maine you
must write; you are meant to indraw from the host of invisibles who are on your wave length. You are at times
'static' because you are caught between the wave lengths
of your real, eternal 'congenials' and your kindred spirits on
earth. Be completely detached, be open to the power longing to flow into you. Your inner urge is unerring when you
are attuned to God. You will one day learn to tune out the
vibrations of those people whose problems are not your
responsibility. Continue to love them compassionately; thus
you will help to lift them and to release them.*

*"I cannot predict a year of no conflict; there will be
many hurdles, but you will be sustained by invisible reinforcement. Light is the answer, light shows the way, light
is the melody of healing for individuals as well as for the
whole world. Be very conscious of Christ as the light within,
as embryonic energy within, which will shatter all that is
not real and release all that is enduring. Let there be light,
laughter and love wherever you three dear ones go.*

"You should dwell more in invisible gatherings than in earthly ones. You will thus become refreshed and a better instrument for God's work. You will also make us happier here. Let us envisage that we of both worlds are flowing together with the waves of light. Countless hosts of angels and illuminated souls hover just over the rim of your busy earth consciousness; we wait and long to turn our love into streams of energy to heal and recreate all areas of darkness."

52

A MESSAGE IN THE PINE WOODS

Franklin and I, and also May, were enjoying another summer in Maine. One night I had a happy dream about my mother, and in the morning the following words from her came into my consciousness. I knew the message was for both of her daughters, and I sensed mother's joy that we were together and attuned to the quiet rhythm of nature as found in our beloved pine woods and in the gentle pulsing of the surrounding tides.

Sebasco Estates, Maine
August 22, 1952

"Children of the Pine Woods, greetings to this day. May peace dwell in your hearts, and may love flow from both silence and activity. This morning my consciousness was directed earthward. The lingering joy you felt upon awakening was but a wave from those of us who hover in constant awareness of you on earth whom we love and wish to serve.

"Many earth-years have gone by since I left on the great adventure, and I often wonder how anyone can grieve or even ponder on the welfare of the 'departed.' We are 'departed' only from dreams we dreamed on earth.

"I have soared and soared, at first being greedy for all wisdom and seeking every channel of truth. Then I thought, 'For what am I making myself ready?' I saw that all my preparation on earth and here was leading toward just one

instant in eternity, one instant which envelops my soul and every other soul. No saint or sinner can live any more than one instant in eternity. Therefore, I left my restlessness of spirit and joined in an outpouring Te Deum of love for our Creator. It was as if I were a meadow lark singing on a treetop. I cannot describe it to you, my children, the joy, the ecstasy of it. That is all life is—a joy—a song to God for our life within.

"Remember that worry, too much activity, too much comfort and too much weariness mock God, and God shall not be mocked. We praise God in tranquility and prayer, never in those things which bring confusion. Do not conform too accurately to man-made standards. Do not give too much importance to earth desires, for they never fully satisfy. Worldly success, fame and fortune—these all pass away. Humility, selflessness, peace, joy and love form the true scaffolding upon which time builds the indestructible mansions.

"We rejoice at your upward climb. That is earth life, a slow ascension. Feet often stumble, knees give way, but eyes are alight because of the urgent calling of Christ. Do you weep when a child falls down and bumps its head? I do not weep when you, my children, are brought level to earth through disappointment, illness or self-entangling circumstances. These are lessons which must be learned, and a new area of unfoldment opens because of them. Rejoice at humiliations, frustrations and defeats, for they mean that He who knows all knows your inner capacity to rise again.

"The world is full of dark shadows. We are urging earth souls to shine radiantly and steadily, rather than in a fickle, flickering way. Only the consecrated and the illumined are able to bring light again into lost and darkened minds. Each of you on earth has a purpose and an inner guide to

keep his light burning. Never let that light go out. Forces
are interpenetrating many planes, some for good, some for
evil. Do not fight dark forces either in individual hearts and
minds or in national ones. Never fight anything, even
selfishness, doubt and strange impulses within yourself. Do
not resist them; rather, ignore them, bless them and re-
nounce them. Look at the ever increasing power of good,
not at evil which will one day be overcome.

"Man should be humble and repentant for his lack of
love and gratitude to the Creator. The world's sickness is
God's warning to return to His ways, just as pain in the
body is a warning to seek physical renewal. Only as man,
falling on his knees in humility, repents of his willfulness,
ignorance and sin will he become awakened to God.

"This is no personal message. Each of you may interpret
it for yourself. I no longer think in the way I did on earth.
There are no relationships on this plane except as we choose
to recall and relive them. Love is the bond, love which is
never personal or static, never enfolding one person, family
or nation, but embracing all.

"Your earth minds become your spiritual auras. Not
what you do, say or dream, but what you think, becomes
your permanent ego. Think on kindness, patience, tolerance,
forgiveness, selflessness, gentleness and beauty; then your
armor of the day will be a mantle of protection against
negative thoughts and conditions. Harmony and health will
come only when your daily armor is strong enough to with-
stand temptations.

"I came in your dreams to assure you that we are tread-
ing together the pathway of light. We here still have to un-
clutter earth errors and often have to redirect our course
more accurately toward the universal flight. I send you all
not only a mother's love, constant as the stars, but a more

intense love. It is a love in which personality is sublimated to truth, truth which liberates man from self. Be alive with laughter and joy, my children. Be with me in this flight of eternal freedom and love."

53

LIGHTED SOULS

One cold September morning in our Maine cottage, I awoke early to discover that an insistent urge to write was forcing me to begin my day earlier than usual. I very much wanted to go back to sleep sheltered in my warm bed from both the cold and the demands of spirit-bidding. However, the pushing of inner thoughts conquered my desire for warmth and rest; soon I was sitting up in bed, with teeth chattering and with cold fingers grasping a pencil which was flying across the pages of a notebook to scribble the following message.

Sebasco Estates, Maine
September 15, 1953

"Awake and arise to the glory of transcendency! Around you are the angelic ones, they who walk among midget men but who rise in spiritual stature above them. They who touch the immense life abounding in dimensions as yet little heralded to human ears.

"These friends are near; never do you know when you may be brushing shoulders lightly against them as you pass through the day's commonplace experiences. They are eager and alert to human desires. They bear the mark of the Christ, the same Jesus who came to bring the oil of love to fill the lanterns of earth life that men might see beyond the misty shadows of earth darkness into the world of spirit, where He is the center of all creation. Christ shines with

the radiance of absolute love, and this love is God. The spiritual bond between feet of clay and wings of spirit is the Christ-centered man or woman.

"Search, as you pass along this life journey, for lighted souls. By your own light shall you perceive and know them. By your loving search shall you unveil them from amidst the many good men. Man is often so absorbed in the mechanics of daily living that he cannot see life's full glory. God's Glory is the real, the hidden, treasure buried amidst the unreal, the cluttered, the transient. Look up and above what seems to be; look up, as your hearts insistently bid you, into smiling reality, into life complete and endless.

"Always be grateful for those things which stifle or frustrate human effort, for they provide new sights with which to behold the harmony of heaven. Do not wait for mankind or conditions to change; do not wait for any state of body, mind or soul to change. Bless your troubles and dream great dreams beyond them. Bathe them in a clear, crystal pool of gratitude and praise until their seeming reality slinks away and the soul becomes resplendent. See the perfect good, feel the perfect love, in everything which binds you, in every relationship toward man and the universe. For one instant is long enough to hold all eternity if man could but realize it, accept it, and draw this truth into his being. In eternity there is only love, and in the heart of love is perfect freedom."

54

WHISPERING ROCK

Not far from our cottage at Sebasco some years ago I discovered, deep in the woods, a rock formation which bore unusual resemblance to an altar. Set amidst towering pines, with its background of soft moss and scalloped ferns, with a silently flowing brook nearby, here indeed was a place of worship not built by human hands. Strange to some ears may be the fact that I was led to this place of almost unearthly beauty and great peace entirely by the promptings of intuition. Once found, I instantly recognized my woods altar as a place of deep meaning for me; instinctively, I sensed its throbbing spiritual overtones and its powerful closeness to reality. "Whispering Rock" became its name because of the murmuring of the pines, of the sea and of nature herself.

"Whispering Rock" quickly grew to be one of my favorite spots at Sebasco, and I often went there for inspiration and renewal. To honor our Lord we built a small birch cross for the altar; then we added to nature's beauty by planting more of her wild ferns, wood mosses and tiny violets. Surrounded by peace, beauty and quiet, I loved to sit or lie on the large rocky ledge above the altar. Meditation and prayer seemed natural as breathing in the cathedral-like stillness; also many messages and poems have been written through me in that place so charged with life-essence. Full of vital force, "Whispering Rock" seemed to emanate new strength and healing.

Many people we brought there sensed something rare and sacred. Voices were lowered to become more in tune with the reverent atmosphere. At the altar, the richest privilege of discipleship has come to us several times when others have there given their lives to Christ.

Our dismay in 1953 may be imagined when we discovered that the woods property on which the altar stood had been sold to a paper company. Woodsmen cut down trees everywhere and stripped the entire section of its protecting pines. Death and destruction appeared to have taken over; dead brush and stumps gave silent, effective evidence of the fact. Many who loved those woods could no longer bear to walk through them, but something made me keep returning to my beloved ledge.

Despite all the wood-cutting operations, despite the felling of trees beside and above the altar, the cross still stood as a triumphant symbol.

The next writing came at "Whispering Rock" that fall just before time for us to leave Maine and return home. The visible signs of death and decay all about me were used to emphasize its message of hope and victory as pertaining to man and the larger but related areas of life. "I am the resurrection and the life, and he that believeth in me, though he were dead, yet shall he live."

Once again, in a little different vein, the oneness of all life is stressed. Today as I write the cross still stands on our altar, despite three later hurricanes and many of Maine's rugged winters. Furthermore, in convincing witness to eternal truth, "a new cycle of fresh vitality" has brought greenness back to our woods. New growth, new glory of nature is burying desolation and restoring natural beauty.

Sebasco Estates, Maine
October 1, 1953

"Dear Mom:

"All man's greed, hate and destruction cannot change the tide of destiny, which is God's love manifesting in all Creation.

"Man's eyes can see the havoc wrought to sacred beauty, but only man's inner seeing and knowing senses new life and new grandeur seeded everywhere amidst this desolation. Even in the cold debris of death is the glorious, pulsating, healing renewal of what God has made and has ordained shall be. Love is constantly renewing and healing all which is less than perfect.

"Death is only the beginning of a new cycle of fresh vitality. One must die to command new life. One must continually see all nature die to enrich the seeds of new life. There is no death except in the consciousness which limits all to the physical senses.

"The substance from which all was and is continually being created is infinite energy. It gives the lift, the love and the laughter to existence. When one sees the foreverness of existence, the oneness of all life (past, present and future) as an expression of or an offshoot from the main source of being, one understands that this life substance is the unseen power of the universe. It is the very mind of God and yet is available to any one who claims it.

"As like attracts like, so does life attract life. Men who deliberately, or through ignorance, cut themselves off from their own source become like dead-end streams and thus fail to fulfill their true heritage and destiny. To express the heart and love of our Creator, even as He expressed His own Heart of Perfection to make this earth planet a work to glorify Him, is our destiny.

"*Dissolve here, in this sanctuary, any feeling of separation from your own source.*

"*As the sun pours into your physical body, so should you feel pouring into your spirit the healing love and the perfection of God's supply of wisdom and grace. Rather than asking for healing, ask for God's permeating infusion of Light; with praise and thanksgiving, rest in the glory of peace and oneness with all that is.*

"*God-speed to this day and to this swiftly passing summer cycle. Divine purpose is being expressed, even though you cannot see it. Gladly, joyfully be lifted into higher strata. Human will or human desire has no place or part in a true disciple's living schedule. Be completely sensitive to the song echoed from Divine instrumentation. Listen daily for the melodies until they become automatic recordings. An echo knows not what it is echoing, yet it is perfect in timing and reproduction. I ask you to be an earthly echo of God's voice. Go in peace, for you are now renewed.*"

55

THE TRIUMPHANT WAY

This final writing came on Mothers' Day, 1954, while Franklin and his sister, Polly, and I were in church together. Having no children of her own, Polly had been like a second mother to Lowell. In his younger days she had spent many hours reading to her nephew, and the shared delight of those early years deepened into a close relationship of mutual understanding and affection as Lowell approached manhood. Therefore, especially appropriate is Lowell's loving reference to Polly on this Mothers' Day, which came just before Franklin and I were to start out for another summer in Maine. The warm personal tone of this message, its prophetic lines and its emphasis on total commitment of our lives to God make it a natural summation of Lowell's main points to us throughout the years.

Christ Church
Coronado, California
May 2, 1954

"Yes, Mom and Dad, I am close to you again to wish you a happy day and a happy trip back to Maine. On Mothers' Day I am always near, and you can feel my vibration stirring within your soul.

"Now is the time for the tide's turning for the world. Great upheavals and changes are to take place. Be prepared in your own and in national life; yet, be not afraid.

All is part of the new cycle preceding a better world. Hold fast to all the faith you have. Love all phases of existence. Threads of hope, joy and life eternal are being woven through all that transpires.

"*Hosts of lighted ones lead you forth, you and all who love God's divine purposes, you who serve and love Him Who eternally serves and loves His own. The time is approaching for the balancing power of divine Love to hasten the ultimate choice of individuals. The time is coming when the true must unite against the false and selfish.*

"*I ask you to help every soul who comes into your life to see the necessity for choosing God's way; pray that all who enter into your consciousness may recognize God's immense Good. It is no longer possible to be lukewarm or to see with double vision; it is no longer possible to play on the world's team and on God's team at the same time. All must choose as light and darkness go into the last cycles of the death struggle.*

"*From my present state of being I see at an angle a little beyond earth vision. As our minds here become more illuminated by clearer perceptions, yours will become more quickened and receptive, with love and wisdom taking control. Then will you intuit the great multitude of consecrated souls leading the way to victory.*

"*I love you, I love the love in you all. Aunt Polly, I love you, too. I touch your heads now, in this Christ-filled sanctuary, with a blessing and a prayer. Go forth, trusting, believing, knowing that, no matter what outward signs are—, all is well. God is triumphant and vitally present wherever and whenever the human soul touches Him in love and prayer.*

"*Peace and joy to your trip and to every experience of the coming days. Praise and adore the one God, the God*

of mercy and love, Who holds each soul tenderly in the
palm of His Hands.

"Mom, my Mom, live joyfully, patiently and creatively.
You and Dad have made me happy and proud. I love you
forever."

As we turn from Lowell's concluding message, we reach
out to the unfaltering love which is expressed through him.
In the oneness of life, we long for continued outreach with
Lowell and the spirit world toward the Light of all Lights.
Just as life and love never end, so the mother and son story
portrayed in this book shall never end. I believe that all
that has gone before in my life, as in your life, is but a tiny
prologue. All reality lies before us, and at last we shall all
rejoice together in one vast chorus of praise and adoration.